MW00355078

TSI MATH PRACTICE TESTS

**Texas Success Initiative Assessment
Math Study Guide with
300 Problems and Solutions**

TSI Math Practice Tests: Texas Success Initiative Assessment Math Study Guide with 300 Problems and Solutions

© COPYRIGHT 2017–2018

Exam SAM Study Aids & Media dba www.examsam.com

ISBN-13: 978-0-9998087-9-5

ISBN-10: 0-9998087-9-6

The drawings in this publication are for illustration purposes only. They are not drawn to an exact scale.

Disclaimer: TSI (Texas Success Initiative) is a registered trademark of the College Entrance Examination Board, which is neither affiliated with nor endorses this publication.

Editor's note: This publication is the second edition of our book entitled: *TSI Math Practice Tests: Texas Success Initiative Assessment Math Study Guide with 250 Problems and Solutions.*

The pagination and layout of the second edition are identical to that of the first edition. The second edition contains 50 new questions that have been placed at the end of the material from the first edition.

TABLE OF CONTENTS

HOW TO USE THIS PUBLICATION

The problems in this study guide require knowledge of elementary algebra and of arithmetic operations, such as addition, subtraction, multiplication, division, percentages, and decimals.

You may feel that you need to review arithmetic and elementary algebra before you try the practice problems in this book.

If so, you should try our free practice exercises in arithmetic and elementary algebra first.

The free review problems can be found at: www.examsam.com

As you work through this study guide, you will notice that practice test questions 1 to 50 provide study tips after each question.

The format of the first set of practice test questions introduces all of the concepts on the exam. This will help you learn the strategies and formulas that you need to answer all of the types of questions on the actual examination.

You can refer back to the formulas and tips introduced in part 1 as you work through the remaining material in the book.

Ideally, you should try to memorize the formulas and tips before you complete the remaining practice test questions in the book.

The solutions and explanations for all of the questions are provided after the 250th question.

The answer key is provided at the end of the book.

TSI Math Practice Test Set 1 – Questions 1 to 50

Manipulating Roots

1) Which of the answers below is equal to the following radical expression? $\sqrt{50}$

A) $1 \div 50$ B) $2\sqrt{25}$ C) $2\sqrt{5}$ D) $5\sqrt{2}$

> Step 1: Factor the number inside the square root sign. Step 2: Look to see if any of the factors are perfect squares. In this case, the only factor that is a perfect square is 25. Step 3: Find the square root of 25 then simplify.

2) $\sqrt{36} + 4\sqrt{72} - 2\sqrt{144} = ?$

A) $2\sqrt{36}$ B) $2\sqrt{252}$ C) $18 + 24\sqrt{2}$ D) $-18 + 24\sqrt{2}$

> Step 1: Find the common factors that are perfect squares. Step 2: Factor the amounts inside each of the radical signs and simplify.

3) $\sqrt{7} \times \sqrt{11} = ?$

A) $\sqrt{77}$ B) $\sqrt{18}$ C) $7\sqrt{11}$ D) $11\sqrt{7}$

> Step 1: Multiply the numbers inside the radical signs. Step 2: Put this product inside a radical symbol for your answer.

4) Express as a rational number: $\sqrt[3]{\dfrac{216}{27}}$

A) 3   B) 2   C) $\dfrac{7}{3}$ D) $\sqrt[3]{2}$

> Step 1: Find the cube roots of the numerator and denominator to eliminate the radical. Step 2: Simplify further if possible. The cube root is a number that equals the required product when multiplied by itself two times.

Manipulating Exponents

5) $7^5 \times 7^3 = ?$

A) 7^8 B) 7^{15} C) 14^8 D) 49^8

> If the base number is the same, you need to add the exponents when multiplying, but keep the base number the same as before.

6) $xy^6 \div xy^3 = ?$

A) xy^{18} B) xy^3 C) x^2y^3 D) xy^2

> If the base number is the same, you need to subtract the exponents when dividing, but keep the base number the same as before.

7) A rocket flies at a speed of 1.7×10^5 miles per hour for 2×10^{-1} hours. How far has this rocket gone?
A) 340,000 miles   B) 34,000 miles   C) 3,400 miles   D) 340 miles

Step 1: Add the exponents to multiply the 10's. Step 2: Multiply the miles per hour by the number of hours to get the distance traveled. Step 3: Then multiply these two results together to solve the problem.

8) $\sqrt{x^{\frac{5}{7}}} = ?$

A) $\dfrac{5x}{7}$ B) $\left(\sqrt[5]{x}\right)^7$ C) $\left(7\sqrt{x}\right)^5$ D) $\left(\sqrt[7]{x}\right)^5$

Step 1: Put the base number inside the radical sign. Step 2: The denominator of the exponent is the nth root of the radical. Step 3: The numerator is the new exponent.

9) $x^{-5} = ?$

A) $\dfrac{1}{x^{-5}}$ B) $\dfrac{1}{x^5}$ C) $-5x$ D) $\dfrac{1}{5x}$

Step 1: Set up a fraction, where 1 is the numerator. Step 2: Put the term with the exponent in the denominator, but remove the negative sign on the exponent.

10) $62^0 = ?$

A) -62 B) 0 C) 1 D) 62

Any non-zero number raised to the power of zero is equal to 1.

Simplifying Rational Algebraic Expressions

11) $\dfrac{b + \frac{2}{7}}{\frac{1}{b}} = ?$

A) $b^2 + \dfrac{7}{2}$ B) $2b + \dfrac{7}{2}$ C) $b^2 + \dfrac{2b}{7}$ D) $\dfrac{b}{b + \frac{2}{7}}$

Step 1: When the expression has fractions in both the numerator and denominator, treat the line in the main fraction as the division symbol. Step 2: Invert the fraction that was in the denominator and multiply.

12) $\dfrac{x^2}{x^2 + 2x} + \dfrac{8}{x} = ?$

A) $\dfrac{x + 8x + 16}{x^2 + 2x}$ B) $\dfrac{x^2 + 8}{x^2 + 3x}$ C) $\dfrac{8x^2 + 16x}{x^3}$ D) $\dfrac{x^2 + 8x + 16}{x^2 + 2x}$

2

Factoring Polynomials

13) Perform the operation and simplify: $\dfrac{2a^3}{7} \times \dfrac{3}{a^2} = ?$

A) $\dfrac{6a}{7}$

B) $\dfrac{5a^3}{7a^2}$

C) $\dfrac{2a^6}{21}$

D) $\dfrac{21}{2a^6}$

14) $\dfrac{8x + 8}{x^4} \div \dfrac{5x + 5}{x^2} = ?$

A) $\dfrac{5x^2}{8}$

B) $\dfrac{8}{5x^2}$

C) $\dfrac{3x+3}{x^2}$

D) $\dfrac{x^2 + 8x + 8}{x^4 + 5x + 5}$

Expanding Polynomials

15) Simplify the following equation: $(x + 4y)^2$

A) $2(x + 8y)$

B) $2x + 8y$

C) $x^2 + 8xy^2 + 16y^2$

D) $x^2 + 8xy + 16y^2$

Linear Equations

16) A mother has noticed that the more sugar her child eats, the more her child sleeps at night. Which of the following graphs best illustrates the relationship between the amount of sugar the child consumes and the child's amount of sleep?

A)

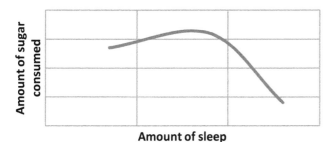

B)

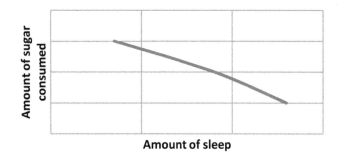

C)

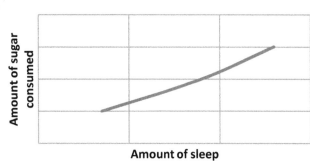

D)

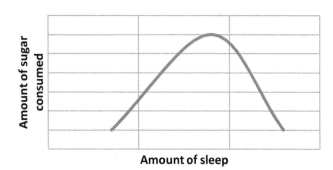

You will need to know the difference between positive linear relationships and negative linear relationships for the exam. In a positive linear relationship, an increase in one variable causes an increase in the other variable, meaning that the line will point upwards from left to right.

In a negative linear relationship, an increase in one variable causes a decrease in the other variable, meaning that the line will point downwards from left to right.

Algebraic Functions

17) The graph of a linear equation is shown below. Which one of the tables of values best represents the points on the graph?

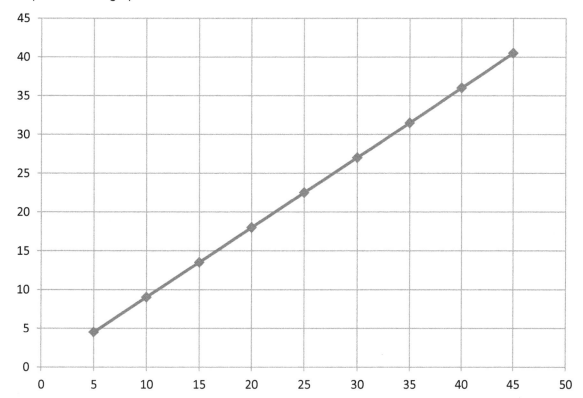

A)

x	y
5	5
10	10
15	15
20	20

B)

x	y
5	4
10	8
15	12
20	16

C)

x	y
5	4.5
10	9
15	13.5
20	18

D)

x	y
5	9
10	13
15	15
20	20

This is an example of an exam question involving algebraic functions. You will have questions on algebraic, polynomial, exponential, and logarithmic functions on your exam. A function expresses the mathematical relationship between x and y. So, a certain recurring mathematical operation on x will yield the output of y. Step 1: Look carefully at the point that is furthest to the left on the graph. You will be able to eliminate several of the answer choices because they will not state this first coordinate correctly.
Step 2: Try to work out the relationship between the coordinates of the first point to those of the next point on the line. Use the horizontal and vertical grid lines on the graph to help you.

Quadratic Equations

18) Simplify: $(x - y)(x + y)$

A) $x^2 - 2xy - y^2$ B) $x^2 + 2xy - y^2$ C) $x^2 + y^2$ D) $x^2 - y^2$

Use the FOIL method on quadratic equations like this one when the instructions tell you to simplify.

Linear Inequalities

19) $50 - \dfrac{3x}{5} \geq 41$, then $x \leq$?

A) 15   B) 25   C) 41   D) 50

Step 1: Isolate the whole numbers to one side of the inequality. Step 2: Get rid of the fraction by multiplying each side by 5. Step 3: Divide to simplify further. Step 4: Isolate the variable to solve.

20) The cost of one wizfit is equal to y. If $x - 2 > 5$ and $y = x - 2$, then the cost of 2 wizfits is greater than which one of the following?

A) $x - 2$ B) $x - 5$ C) $y + 5$ D) 10

Look to see if the inequality and the equation have any variables or terms in common. In this problem, both the inequality and the equation contain $x - 2$. The cost of one wizfit is represented by y, and y is equal to $x - 2$. So, we can substitute values from the equation to the inequality.

Quadratic Inequalities

21) Solve for x: $x^2 - 9 < 0$

A) $x < -3$ or $x > 3$
B) $x > -3$ or $x < 3$
C) $x < -3$ or $x < 3$
D) $x > -3$ or $x > 3$

For quadratic inequality problems like this one, you need to factor the inequality first. We know that the factors of -9 are: -1×9; -3×3; 1×-9. We do not have a term with only the x variable, so we need factors that add up to zero. $-3 + 3 = 0$. So, try to solve the problem based on these facts. Be sure to check your work when you have found a solution.

Systems of Equations

22) What ordered pair is a solution to the following system of equations?

$x + y = 7$
$xy = 12$

A) $(2, 6)$
B) $(6, 2)$
C) $(4, 2)$
D) $(3, 4)$

Step 1: Look at the multiplication equation and find the factors of 12. Step 2: Add the factors in each set together to see if they equal 7 to solve the addition in the first equation.

23) Solve by elimination: $3x + 3y = 15$ and $x + 2y = 8$

A) $x = -18$ and $y = 13$
B) $x = -2$ and $y = 3$
C) $x = 2$ and $y = 3$
D) $x = 3$ and $y = 2$

Step 1: Look at the x term of the first equation, which is $3x$. In order to eliminate the x variable, we need to multiply the second equation by 3. Step 2: Subtract this result from the first equation to solve.

Other Algebraic Concepts

24) Find the value of the following:

$$\sum_{x=3}^{5} x - 1$$

A) 2
B) 3
C) 4
D) 9

Step 1: You need to perform the operation at the right-hand side of the sigma sign for x = 3. Step 2: We repeat the operation until we use the number at the top of the sigma sign. Step 3: Add the three individual results together to get your answer.

25) If Đ is a special operation defined by $(x \text{ Đ } y) = (30x \div 9y)$ and $(3 \text{ Đ } y) = 10$, then $y = ?$

A) 1
B) 3
C) 9
D) 30

We have the special operation defined as $(x Ð y) = (30x ÷ 9y)$. Looking at the relationship between the left-hand side and the right-hand side of this equation, we can determine the operations that need to be performed on any new equation containing the operation Ð and variables x and y. For our problem, the new equation will be carried out as follows: Operation Ð is division; the number or variable before the special operation symbol is multiplied by 30; and the number or variable after the special operation symbol is multiplied by 9.

Logarithmic Functions

26) $2 = \log_8 64$ is equivalent to which of the following?

A) 2^8 B) 8^2 C) 64^2 D) 64^8

Solve by substituting values into the equation. $x = \log_y Z$ is the same as $y^x = Z$

Plane and Coordinate Geometry

27) The triangle in the illustration below is an isosceles triangle. What is the measurement of ∠B?

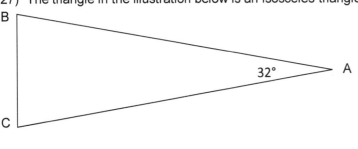

A) 32°   B) 45°   C) 74°   D) 148°

Step 1: Deduct the measurement of angle A from 180° to find out the total degrees of the two other angles. Step 2: Since we have an isosceles triangle, the other two angles are equal in measure.

You should know these principles on angles and triangles for your exam:

The sum of all three angles in any triangle must be equal to 180 degrees.

An isosceles triangle has two equal sides and two equal angles.

An equilateral triangle has three equal sides and three equal angles.

Angles that have the same measurement in degrees are called congruent angles.

Equilateral triangles are sometimes called congruent triangles.

Two angles are supplementary if they add up to 180 degrees. This means that when the two angles are placed together, they will form a straight line on one side.

Two angles are complementary (sometimes called adjacent angles) if they add up to 90 degrees. This means that the two angles will form a right angle.

When two parallel lines are cut by a transversal (a straight line that runs through both of the parallel lines), 4 pairs of opposite (non-adjacent) angles are formed and 4 pairs of corresponding angles are formed. The opposite angles will be equal in measure, and the corresponding angles will also be equal in measure.

A parallelogram is a four-sided figure in which opposite sides are parallel and equal in length. Each angle will have the same measurement as the angle opposite to it, so a parallelogram has two pairs of opposite angles.

The sides of a 30° - 60° - 90° triangle are in the ratio of 1:$\sqrt{3}$: 2.

28) The central angle in the circle below is 90° and is subtended by an arc which is 8π centimeters in length. How many centimeters long is the radius of this circle?

Arc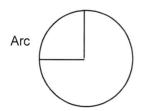

A) 32   B) 16   C) 8π D) 8

When working with arcs, you can calculate the radius or diameter of a circle if you have the measurement of a central angle and the length of the arc subtending the central angle. You will also need the formula for circumference: Circumference = $\pi \times$ radius $\times$ 2. You can think of arc length as part of the circumference.

29) A field is 100 yards long and 32 yards wide. What is the area of the field in square yards?

A) 160   B) 320   C) 1600   D) 3200

Area of a circle: $\pi \times r^2$ (radius squared)
Area of a square or rectangle: length × width
Area of a triangle: (base × height) ÷ 2

30) If a circle has a diameter of 6, what is the circumference of the circle?

A) 6π B) 12π C) 24π D) 36π

Diameter = radius × 2
Remember that the formula for the circumference of a circle is $\pi \times$ diameter.

31) If a circle with center (−5, 5) is tangent to the x axis in the standard (x, y) coordinate plane, what is the diameter of the circle?

A) −5   B) −10   C) 5   D) 10

Diameter is the measurement across the entire width of a circle. Diameter is always double the radius. If the center of a circle (x, y) is tangent to the x axis, then both of the following conditions are true: [1] The point of tangency is equal to (x, 0) and [2] The distance between (x, y) and (x, 0) is equal to the radius.

32) XY is 4 inches long and XZ is 5 inches long. What is the area of right triangle XYZ?

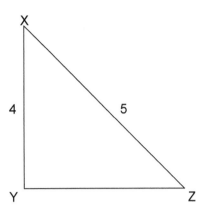

A) 3   B) 5   C) 6   D) 10

Step 1: Use the Pythagorean theorem to find the length of line segment XZ.
Hypotenuse length $C = \sqrt{A^2 + B^2}$
Step 2: Calculate the area of the triangle: (base × height) ÷ 2

33) In the figure below, ∠Y is a right angle and ∠X = 60°. If line segment YZ is 5 units long, then how long is line segment XY?

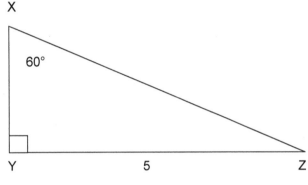

A) 5 units   B) 6 units   C) 15 units   D) $\frac{5}{\sqrt{3}}$ units

Triangle XYZ is a 30° - 60° - 90° triangle.
Using the Pythagorean theorem, its sides are therefore in the ratio of $1 : \sqrt{3} : 2$.

34) What is the perimeter of a rectangle that has a length of 17 and a width of 4?

A) 21   B) 34   C) 42   D) 68

In order to calculate the perimeter of squares and rectangles, you need to use the perimeter formula:
(length × 2) + (width × 2)

35) If the radius of a circle is 4 and the radians of the subtended angle measure $^\pi/_4$, what is the length of the arc subtending the central angle?

A) $^\pi/_4$ B) $^\pi/_8$ C) π D) 4π

Radians can be illustrated by the diagram and formulas that follows.

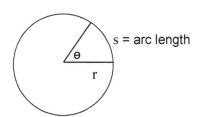

s = arc length

θ = the radians of the subtended angle
s = arc length
r = radius
The following formulas can be used for calculations with radians:
θ = s ÷ r
s = r θ

Also remember these useful formulas.
π × 2 × radian = 360°
π × radian = 180°
π ÷ 2 × radian = 90°
π ÷ 4 × radian = 45°
π ÷ 6 × radian = 30°

36) A cone has a height of 9 inches and a radius at its base of 4 inches. What is the volume of this cone?
A) 13π B) 24π C) 48π D) 144π

Box volume: volume = base × width × height
Cone volume: (π × radius^2 × height) ÷ 3
Cylinder volume: π × radius^2 × height
Pyramid volume = (W × L × H) ÷ 3

37) If store A is represented by the coordinates (−4, 2) and store B is represented by the coordinates (8,−6), and store A and store B are connected by a line segment, what is the midpoint of this line?

A) (2, 2) B) (2, −2) C) (−2, 2) D) (−2, −2)

The midpoint of two points on a two-dimensional graph is calculated by using the midpoint formula:
$(x_1 + x_2) ÷ 2$, $(y_1 + y_2) ÷ 2$

38) What is the distance between (2, 3) and (6, 7)?

A) 4   B) 16   C) $\sqrt{16}$ D) $\sqrt{32}$

The distance formula is used to calculate the linear distance between two points on a two-dimensional graph. The two points are represented by the coordinates (x_1, y_1) and (x_2, y_2).

$d = \sqrt{(x_2 - x_1)^2 + (y_2 - y_1)^2}$

---

39) The measurements of a mountain can be placed on a two dimensional linear graph on which $x = 5$ and $y = 315$. If the line crosses the y axis at 15, what is the slope of this mountain?

A) 60   B) 63   C) 300   D) 315

The slope formula: $m = \dfrac{y_2 - y_1}{x_2 - x_1}$

The slope-intercept formula: $y = mx + b$, where m is the slope and b is the y intercept.

---

40) Find the x and y intercepts of the following equation: $x^2 + 2y^2 = 144$

A) (12, 0) and (0, $\sqrt{72}$)   B) (0, 12) and ($\sqrt{72}$, 0)

C) (0, $\sqrt{72}$) and (0, 12)   D) (12, 0) and ($\sqrt{72}$, 0)

For questions about x and y intercepts, substitute 0 for y in the equation provided. Then substitute 0 for x to solve the problem.

Data Analysis, Statistics, and Probability

41) Aleesha rolls a fair pair of six-sided dice. Each die has values from 1 to 6. She rolls an even number on her first roll. What is the probability that she will roll an odd number on her next roll?

A) $\frac{1}{2}$ B) $\frac{1}{6}$ C) $\frac{2}{6}$ D) $\frac{6}{11}$

This is a question on calculating basic probability. First of all, calculate how many items there are in total in the data set, which is also called the "sample space" or (S). Then reduce the data set if further items are removed. Probability can be expressed as a fraction. The number of items available in the total data set at the time of the event goes in the denominator. The chance of the desired outcome, which is also referred to as the event or (E), goes in the numerator of the fraction. You can determine the chance of the event by calculating how many possibilities there are for the desired outcome.

---

42) A student receives the following scores on his exams during the semester: 89, 65, 75, 68, 82, 74, 86. What is the mean of his scores?

A) 24   B) 74   C) 75   D) 77

The arithmetic mean is the same thing as the arithmetic average. In order to calculate the mean, add up the values of all of the items in the set, and then divide by the number of items.

43) Members of a weight loss group report their individual weight loss to the group leader every week. During the week, the following amounts in pounds were reported: 1, 1, 3, 2, 4, 3, 1, 2, and 1. What is the mode of the weight loss for the group?

A) 1 pound   B) 2 pounds   C) 3 pounds   D) 4 pounds

This is a question on mode. Mode is the value that occurs most frequently in a data set. For example, if 10 students scored 85 on a test, 6 students scored 90, and 4 students scored 80, the mode score is 85.

44) Mark's record of times for the 400 meter freestyle at swim meets this season is: 8.19, 7.59, 8.25, 7.35, and 9.10. What is the median of his times?

A) 7.59   B) 8.19   C) 8.25   D) 8.096

This question is asking you to find the median of a set of numbers. The median is the number that is in the middle of the set when the numbers are in ascending order.

45) A student receives the following scores on her assignments during the term: 98.5, 85.5, 80.0, 97, 93, 92.5, 93, 87, 88, 82. What is the range of her scores?

A) 17.0   B) 18.0   C) 18.5   D) 89.65

This is a question on calculating range. To calculate range, the lowest value in the data set is deducted from the highest value in the data set.

46) Six students in an advanced algebra class got the following grades on a semester test: 99, 98, 74, 69, 87, and 83. What is the variance of these exam scores?

A) 85   B) 125   C) 510   D) 750

The variance measures how far each individual number in a set is from the mean. The variance of a data set is calculated as follows:
Step 1 – Find the arithmetic mean (or average) for the data set.
Step 2 – Calculate the "difference from the mean" for each item in the set. You can calculate the "difference from the mean" by subtracting the mean from each value.
Step 3 – Square the "difference from the mean" for each item by multiplying the value of the item by itself.
Step 4 – Determine the mean of the individual amounts from step 3 above to calculate the variance.

47) What is the standard deviation for the data set in question 46 above?

A) 5   B) 125   C) $5\sqrt{5}$ D) 15,625

Standard deviation measures how spread out the data is, compared to the mean or expected value. The standard deviation is calculated by taking the square root of the variance.

48) If 8 out of 32 students had test scores higher than 90, what score would a student need in order to be in the 75th percentile?

A) 91 or more   B) 90 or more   C) 75 or more   D) 24 or more

> To calculate the percentile for an observation (x), divide the number of observations less than x by the total number of observations. Then multiply this quantity by 100.

49) A zoo has reptiles, birds, quadrupeds, and fish. At the start of the year, they have a total of 1,500 creatures living in the zoo. The pie chart below shows percentages by category for the 1,500 creatures at the start of the year.

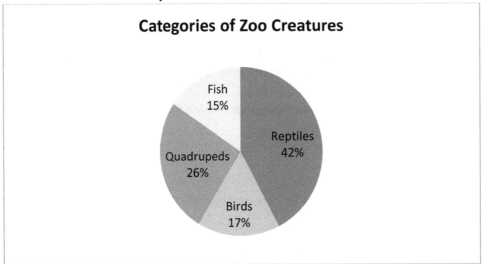

Categories of Zoo Creatures

At the end of the year, the zoo still has 1,500 creatures, but reptiles constitute 40%, birds 23%, and quadrupeds 21%. How many more fish were there at the end of the year than at the beginning of the year?

A) 10   B) 11   C) 15   D) 16

> This question is asking you to interpret a pie chart that shows percentages by category. If you are asked to calculate changes to the data in the categories in the chart, be sure to multiply by the percentages at the beginning of the year and then do a separate calculation using the percentages at the end of the year.

50) The pictograph below shows the number of pizzas sold in one day at a local pizzeria. Cheese pizzas sold for $10 each, pepperoni pizzas sold for $12, and the total sales of all three types of pizza was $310. What is the sales price of one vegetable pizza?

Cheese	▼ ▼ ▼
Pepperoni	▼ ▼
Vegetable	▼

Each ▼ represents 5 pizzas.

A) $5   B) $8   C) $9   D) $10

This is an example of an exam question on interpreting data from pictographs. Each symbol on the pictograph represents a certain quantity of items, so remember to multiply by that amount in order to determine the totals for each group.

51) Solve for x: $x^2 - 5x + 6 \le 0$
A) $2 \ge x \ge 3$
B) $2 \le x \le 3$
C) $x < -3$ or $x < 2$
D) $x > -2$ or $x > 3$

52) $x^2 + xy - y = 254$ and $x = 12$. What is the value of y?
A) 110
B) 10
C) 11
D) 12

53) $(3x + y)(x - 5y) = ?$
A) $3x^2 - 14xy - 5y^2$
B) $3x^2 - 14xy + 5y^2$
C) $3x^2 + 14xy - 5y^2$
D) $3x^2 + 14xy + 5y^2$

54) Factor: $9x^3 - 3x$
A) $3x(3x^2 - 1)$
B) $3x(3x - 1)$
C) $3x(x^2 - 1)$
D) $3x(x - 3)$

55) The perimeter of the square shown below is 36 units. What is the length of line segment JK?

J

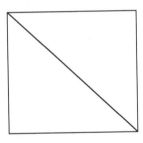

K

A) 9   B) 18   C) $\sqrt{162}$ D) 81

56) The graph of a line is shown on the xy plane below. The point that has the y-coordinate of 45 is not shown. What is the corresponding x-coordinate of that point?

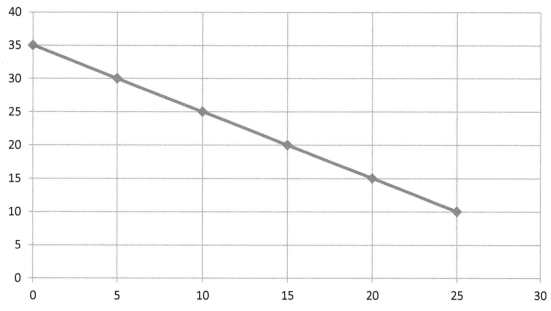

A) –10   B) –5   C) 0   D) 5

57) Simplify: $\sqrt{15} + 3\sqrt{15}$
A) 45   B) $4\sqrt{15}$ C) $2\sqrt{15}$ D) $3\sqrt{30}$

58) $\sqrt{5} \times \sqrt{3}$
A) 15   B) $\sqrt{8}$ C) $\sqrt{15}$ D) $5\sqrt{3}$

59) Which of the following equations is equivalent to $\frac{x}{5} + \frac{y}{2}$?

A) $\frac{x+y}{7}$ B) $\frac{2x+5y}{10}$ C) $\frac{5x+2y}{10}$ D) $\frac{2x+5y}{7}$

60) What equation represents the slope-intercept formula for the following data?

Through (4, 5); $m = -\frac{3}{5}$

A) $y = -\frac{3}{5}x + 5$ B) $y = -\frac{12}{5}x - 5$ C) $y = -\frac{3}{5}x - \frac{37}{5}$ D) $y = -\frac{3}{5}x + \frac{37}{5}$

61) Simplify and perform the operation:

$$\frac{x^2 + 5x + 4}{x^2 + 6x + 5} \times \frac{16}{x + 5}$$

A) $\frac{16x + 64}{x + 5}$ B) $\frac{x + 20}{x + 5}$ C) $\frac{x + 20}{x^2 + 10x + 25}$ D) $\frac{16x + 64}{x^2 + 10x + 25}$

62) Perform the operation and simplify:

$$\frac{8x-8}{x} \div \frac{3x-3}{6x^2}$$

A) $\frac{3x^2-3x}{48x^3-48x^2}$ B) $\frac{5x-5}{6x^2}$ C) $\frac{8(x-1)\times 6x^2}{x \times 3(x-1)}$ D) $16x$

63) $(25x)^0$

A) 0   B) 5   C) 1   D) 25

64) $4^{11} \times 4^8$ = ?

A) 16^{19} B) 4^{19} C) 8^{19} D) 4^{88}

65) $\sqrt{8x^4} \cdot \sqrt{32x^6}$ = ?

A) $8\sqrt{32x^{10}}$ B) $16x^{10}$ C) $16x^5$ D) $256x^{10}$

66) The length of a box is 20cm, the width is 15cm, and the height is 25cm, what is the volume of the box?

A) 150   B) 300   C) 750   D) 7500

67) If one leg of a triangle is 5cm and the other leg is 12cm, what is the measurement of the hypotenuse of the triangle?

A) $5\sqrt{12}$cm   B) $12\sqrt{5}$cm   C) $\sqrt{17}$cm   D) 13 cm

68) In the figure below, A and B are parallel lines, and line C is a transversal crossing both A and B. Which angles are equal in measure?

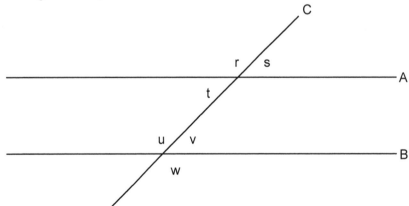

A) ∠r, ∠s, ∠t   B) ∠r, ∠u, ∠v   C) ∠r, ∠u, ∠w   D) ∠r, ∠t, ∠u

69) The central angle in a circle is subtended by an arc which is 3π inches in length. The radius of the circle is 18. What is the measurement of the central angle?

A) 30°   B) 12°   C) 5°   D) 3°

70) Which of the following dimensions would be needed in order to find the area of the figure?

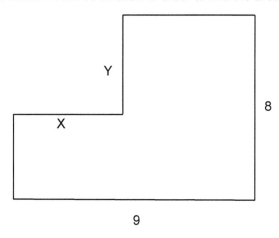

A) X only   B) Y only   C) Both X and Y   D) Either X or Y

71) The figure below shows a right triangular prism. Side AB measures 3.5 units, side AC measures 4 units, and side BD measures 5 units. What amount below best approximates the total surface area of this triangular prism in square units?

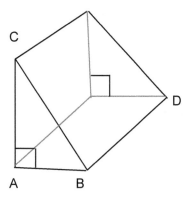

A) 66.5   B) 72.85   C) 74   D) 78.00

72) The base (B) of the cylinder in the illustration shown below is at a right angle to its sides. The radius (R) of the base of cylinder measures 5 centimeters. The height of the cylinder is 14 centimeters. What is the volume of the cylinder?

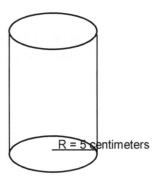

R = 5 centimeters

A) 60π   B) 140π   C) 350π   D) 700π

73) Circle 1 and circle 2 are two concentric circles with radii of $R_1 = 1$ and $R_2 = 2.4$ as shown in the illustration below. Line L forms the diameter of the circles. What is the area of the lined part of the illustration?

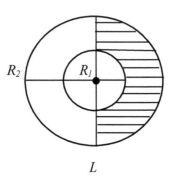

R_2 R_1

L

A) 0.7π   B) 1.4π   C) 2π   D) 2.38π

74) AB and CD are parallel and lengths are provided in units. What is the area of trapezoid ABCD ?

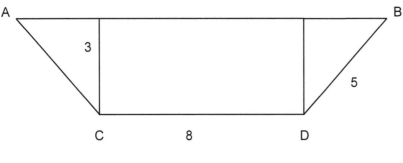

A B
3
5
C   8   D

A) 24   B) 30   C) 34   D) 36

75) In the illustration below, the circle centered at X is internally tangent to the circle centered at Y. The length of line segment XY represents the radius of circle X and is 4 units in length. If the smaller circle passes through the center of the larger circle, what is the area of the larger circle?

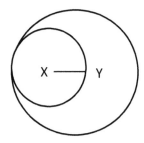

A) 8π   B) 16π   C) 38π   D) 64π

76) A circle has a radius of 12. What is the circumference of the circle?

A) π/12   B) π/24   C) 24π   D) 144π

77) Circle M has a radius of 8, and the area of circle M is 39π greater than the area of circle N. What is the radius of circle N?

A) 5π   B) 5   C) 6   D) 6.5

78) State the x and y intercepts that fall on the straight line represented by the equation: $y = x + 14$
A) (−14, 0) and (0, 14)
B) (0, 14) and (0, −14)
C) (14, 0) and (0, −14)
D) (0, −14) and (14, 0)

79) Find the midpoint of the line segment that connects the points (5, 2) and (7, 4).
A) (6, 3)
B) (3, 6)
C) (3.5, 5.5)
D) (12, 6)

80) Express the following in scientific notation: 1,200,000
A) log1200
B) log1200 × 10³
C) 1.2 × 10⁵
D) 12 × 10⁶

81) The graph below illustrates which of the following functions?

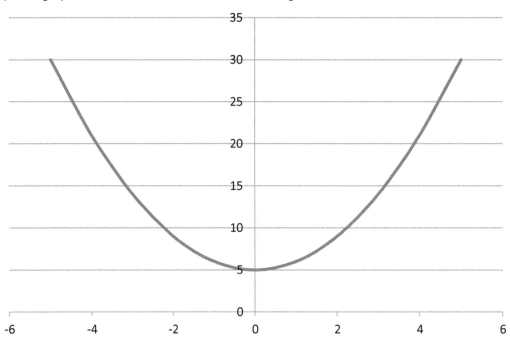

A) $f(x) = x + 5$ B) $f(x) = x - 5$ C) $f(x) = x^2 + 5$ D) $f(x) = x^2 - 5$

82) What is the value of $f_1(2)$ where $f_1(x) = 5^x$?

A) 2^5 B) 10   C) 25   D) 25^2

83) $(-4)^{-3} = ?$

A) –64   B) $-\frac{1}{64}$ C) $\frac{1}{64}$ D) 64

84)   In the right triangle below, the length of AC is 10 units and the length of BC is 8 units. What is the length of AB ?

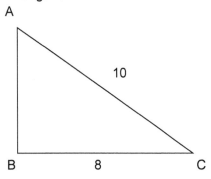

A) 4   B) $\sqrt{164}$ C) 6   D) 7

85) The ages of 5 siblings are: 2, 5, 7, 12, and 14. What is the mean age of the 5 siblings?

A) 8 B) 10 C) 12 D) 14

86) Sam rolls a fair pair of six-sided dice. One of the die is black and the other is red. Each die has values from 1 to 6. What is the probability that Sam will roll a 4 on the red die and a 5 on the black die?

A) $^1/_{36}$ B) $^2/_{36}$ C) $^1/_{12}$ D) $^2/_{12}$

87) In an athletic competition, the maximum possible amount of points was 25 points per participant. The scores for 15 different participants are displayed in the graph below. What was the median score for the 15 participants?

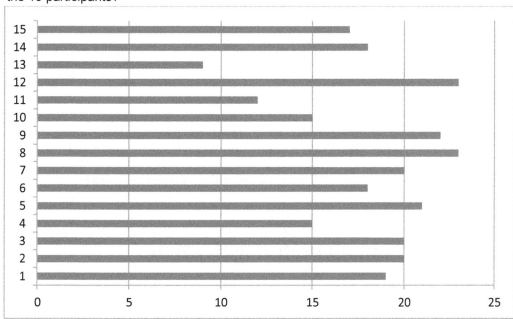

A) 8 B) 12 C) 15 D) 19

88) A plumber charges $100 per job, plus $25 per hour worked. He is going to do 5 jobs this month. He will earn a total of $4,000. How many hours will he work this month?

A) 32 B) 40 C) 140 D) 160

89) $\left(2 + \sqrt{6}\right)^2 = ?$

A) 8 B) $8 + 2\sqrt{6}$ C) $8 + 4\sqrt{6}$ D) $10 + 4\sqrt{6}$

90) The table below shows information on disease by different types. Approximately how many cancer and leukemia patients have not survived?

Disease or Complication	Percentage of patients of this disease or complication type that have survived and total number of patients
Cardiopulmonary and vascular	82% (602,000)
HIV/AIDS	73% (215,000)
Diabetes	89% (793,000)
Cancer and leukemia	48% (231,000)
Premature birth complications	64% (68,000)

A)   24,480
B)   110,880
C)   120,120
D)   231,000

91) The combined total of sales for all three of the companies was greatest during which month of the year?

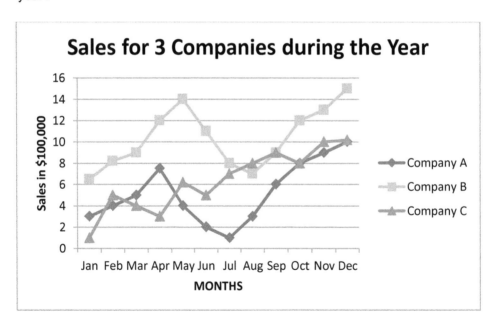

A)   December
B)   November
C)   May
D)   April

92) Calculate the total amount of rainfall for the county that had the least amount of rainfall for all four months in total.

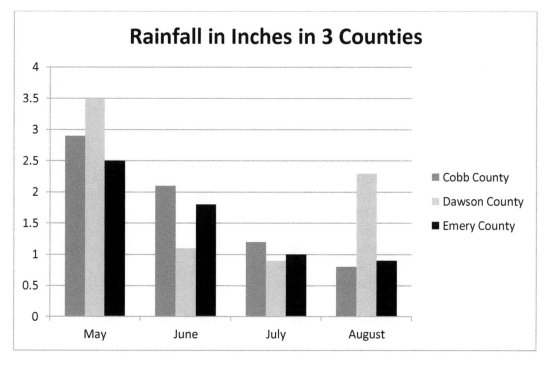

A)   6.2   B) 6.9   C) 7   D) 7.8

93) An owner of a carnival attraction draws teddy bears out of a bag at random to give to prize winners. She has 10 brown teddy bears, 8 white teddy bears, 4 black teddy bears, and 2 pink teddy bears when she opens the attraction at the start of the day. The first prize winner of the day receives a brown teddy bear. What is the probability that the second prize winner will receive a pink teddy bear?

A) $^1/_{24}$ B) $^1/_{23}$ C) $^2/_{24}$ D) $^2/_{23}$

94) Find the median of the following: 2.5, 9.4, 3.1, 1.7, 3.2, 8.2, 4.5, 6.4, 7.8

A) 3.2   B) 4.5   C) 5.2   D) 6.4

95) What is the mode of the numbers in the following list? 1.6, 2.9, 4.5, 2.5, 2.5, 5.1, 5.4

A) 3.5   B) 3.1   C) 3.0   D) 2.5

96) There are 10 cars in a parking lot. Nine of the cars are 2, 3, 4, 5, 6, 7, 9, 10, and 12 years old, respectively. If the average age of the 10 cars is 6 years old, how old is the 10th car?

A) 1 year old   B) 2 years old   C) 3 years old   D) 4 years old

97) An employee at the Department of Motor Vehicles wanted to find the mean of the ten driving theory tests they administered this morning. However, the employee divided the total points from the ten tests by 8, which gave him an erroneous result of 78. What is the correct mean of the ten tests?

A) 97.5   B) 70   C) 62.4   D) 52

98) Toby is going to buy a car. The total purchase price of the car is represented by variable C. He will pay D dollars immediately, and then he will make equal payments (P) each month for a certain number of months (M). Which equation below represents the amount of his monthly payment (P)?

A) $\frac{C-D}{M}$ B) $\frac{C}{M} - D$ C) $\frac{M}{C-D}$ D) $D - \frac{C}{M}$

99) There are three boys in a family, named Alex, Burt, and Zander. Alex is twice as old as Burt, and Burt is one year older than three times the age of Zander. Which of the following statements best describes the relationship between the ages of the boys?
A) Alex is 4 years older than 6 times the age of Zander.
B) Alex is 2 years older than 6 times the age of Zander.
C) Alex is 4 years older than 3 times the age of Zander.
D) Alex is 2 years older than 3 times the age of Zander.

100) The price of a sofa at a local furniture store was x dollars on Wednesday this week. On Thursday, the price of the sofa was reduced by 10% of Wednesday's price. On Friday, the price of the sofa was reduced again by 15% of Thursday's price. Which of the following expressions can be used to calculate the price of the sofa on Friday?
A) (0.75)x   B) (0.10)(0.15)x   C) (0.10)(0.85)x   D) (0.90)(0.85)x

101) Expand the polynomial: $(x - 5)(3x + 8)$
A) $3x^2 - 7x - 40$ B) $3x^2 - 7x + 40$ C) $3x^2 + 23x - 40$ D) $3x^2 + 23x + 40$

102) If $\frac{3}{4}x - 2 = 4$, $x = $?
A) $\frac{8}{3}$ B) $\frac{1}{8}$ C) 8   D) –8

103) Solve for x: $x^2 + 2x - 8 \leq 0$
A) $-4 \geq x \geq 2$ B) $-4 \geq x \leq 2$
C) $-4 \leq x \geq 2$ D) $-4 \leq x \leq 2$

104) If $x - 15 > 0$ and $y = x - 15$, then $y > $?
A) x B) $x + 15$ C) $x - 15$ D) 0

105) 2 inches on a scale drawing represents F feet. Which of the following equations represents $F + 1$ feet on the drawing?

A) $\frac{2(F+1)}{F}$ B) $\frac{(F+1)}{F}$ C) $\frac{2}{F+1}$ D) $\frac{2F}{F+1}$

106) The speed of sound in a recent experiment was 340,000 millimeters per second. How far did the sound travel in 1,000 seconds?
A) 3.4×10^5 millimeters   B) 3.4×10^6 millimeters
C) 3.4×10^7 millimeters   D) 3.4×10^8 millimeters

107) Which of the following is equivalent to the expression $2(x + 2)(x - 3)$ for all values of x?
A) $2x^2 - 2x - 12$ B) $2x^2 - 10x - 6$ C) $2x^2 + 2x - 12$ D) $2x^2 + 10x - 6$

108) Factor the following: $2xy - 6x^2y + 4x^2y^2$
A) $2xy(1 + 3x - 2xy)$ B) $2xy(1 - 3x + 2xy)$ C) $2xy(1 + 3x + 2xy)$ D) $2xy(1 - 3x - 2xy)$

109) A construction company is building new homes on a housing development. It has an agreement with the municipality that H number of houses must be built every 30 days. If H number of houses are not built during the 30 day period, the company has to pay a penalty to the municipality of P dollars per house. The penalty is paid per house for the number of houses that fall short of the 30-day target. If A represents the actual number of houses built during the 30-day period, which equation below can be used to calculate the penalty for the 30-day period?
A) $(H - P) \times 30$ B) $(H - A) \times P$ C) $(A - H) \times 30$ D) $(A - H) \times P$

110) Perform the operation: $(5ab - 6a)(3ab^3 - 4b^2 - 3a)$
A) $15a^2b^4 - 20ab^3 - 15a^2b - 18a^2b^3 - 24ab^2 - 18a^2$
B) $15a^2b^4 - 20ab^3 - 15a^2b - 18a^2b^3 + 24ab^2 + 18a^2$
C) $15a^2b^4 - 20ab^3 - 15a^2b - 18a^2b^3 - 24ab^2 + 18a^2$
D) $15ab^4 - 20ab^3 - 15a^2b - 18a^2b^3 + 24ab^2 + 18a^2$

27

111) Which of the following equations is equivalent to $\frac{x}{5} \div \frac{9}{y}$?

A) $\frac{xy}{45}$

B) $\frac{9x}{5y}$

C) $\frac{1}{9} \times \frac{x}{5y}$

D) $\frac{1}{5} \times \frac{9}{5y}$

112) Which of the following values of x is a possible solution to the inequality?: $-3x + 14 < 5$

A) -3.1

B) 2.80

C) 2.25

D) 3.15

113) $(x - 2y)(2x^2 - y) = ?$

A) $2x^3 - 4x^2y + 2y^2 - xy$

B) $2x^3 + 2y^2 - 5xy$

C) $2x^3 - 4x^2y + 2y^2 + xy$

D) $2x^3 + 4x^2y + 2y^2 - xy$

114) What is the value of the expression $2x^2 + 5xy - y^2$ when $x = 4$ and $y = -3$?

A) -37

B) -19

C) 86

D) 101

115) If $6 + 8(2\sqrt{x} + 4) = 62$, then $\sqrt{x} = ?$

A) 3.25

B) 24

C) $\frac{3}{2}$

D) $\frac{2}{3}$

116) $\sqrt{18} \times \sqrt{8} = ?$

A) $18\sqrt{8}$

B) $\sqrt{26}$

C) $\sqrt{12}$

D) 12

117) If $2(3x - 1) = 4(x + 1) - 3$, what is the value of x?

A) $^3/_2$

B) 3

C) $^2/_3$

D) 2

118) The graph of a linear equation is shown below. Which one of the tables of values best represents the points on the graph?

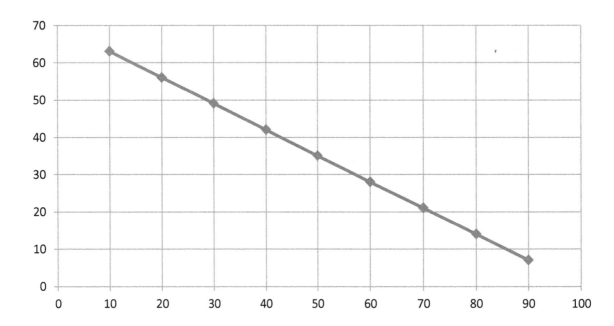

A)

x	y
5	65
10	64
15	63
20	62

B)

x	y
5	68
15	60
25	52
35	54

C)

x	y
10	63
20	56
30	49
40	42

D)

x	y
10	68
20	60
30	52
40	44

119) Triangles FGH and FGJ are right triangles. The lengths of FG, GH, and HJ are provided in units. What is the area of triangle FHJ in square units?

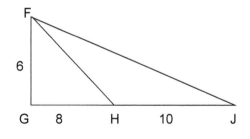

A) 24   B) 30   C) 48   D) 54

120) ABC is an isosceles triangle. Angle DAC is 109° and points A, B, and D are co-linear. What is the measurement of ∠C?

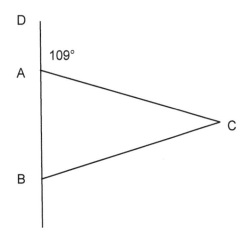

A) 71°   B) 38°   C) 138°   D) 180°

121) If a circle has a diameter of 36, what is the area of the circle?
A) 18π   B) 36π   C) 72π   D) 324π

122) $20 - \frac{3x}{4} \geq 17$, then $x \leq$?
A) –12   B) –4   C) –3   D) 4

123) A rectangular box has a base that is 5 inches wide and 6 inches long. The height of the box is 10 inches. What is the volume of the box?
A) 30   B) 110   C) 150   D) 300

124) Vertex V is the vertex of an angle at the center of a circle. The diameter of the circle is 3. If the angle measures 60 degrees, what is the arc length relating to the central angle?
A) $^{\pi}/_2$ B) $^{\pi}/_4$ C) 2π   D) 4π

125) A vegetable grower wants to put to put wooden fence panels around the outside of her vegetable patch. Each panel is 1 yard in length. The patch is rectangular and is 12 yards long and 10 yards wide. How many panels are needed in order to enclose the vegetable patch?
A) 22   B) 44   C) 100   D) 120

126) Find the volume of a cone which has a radius of 3 and a height of 4.
A) 4π   B) 12π   C) $^{4\pi}/_3$ D) $^{3\pi}/_4$

127) Triangle ABC is a right-angled triangle, where side A and side B form the right angle, and side C is the hypotenuse. If A = 7 and C = 14, what is the length of side B?
A) 2   B) 7   C) $\sqrt{147}$ D) 147

128)

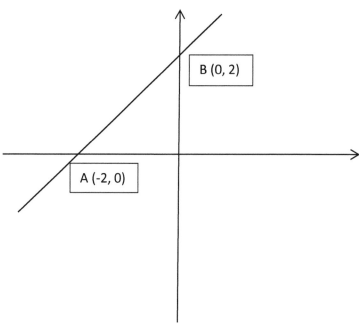

The line in the *xy* plane above is going to be shifted 5 units to the left and 4 units up. What are the coordinates of point B after the shift?

A)   (−5, 6)   B) (5, 6)   C) (5, 4)   D) (−7, 4)

129) A packaging company uses string to secure their packages prior to shipment. The string is tied around the entire length and entire width of the package, as shown in the following illustration:

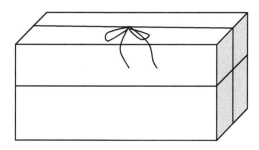

The box is ten inches in height, ten inches in depth, and twenty inches in length. An additional fifteen inches of string is needed to tie a bow on the top of the package. How much string is needed in total in order to tie up the entire package, including making the bow on the top?

A)   80   B) 100   C) 120   D) 135

130) The triangle in the illustration below is an equilateral triangle. What is the measurement in degrees of angle *a*?

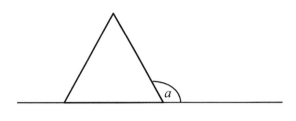

A) 45   B) 60   C) 120   D) 180

131) The radius (R) of circle A is 5 centimeters. The radius of circle B is 3 centimeters. Which of the following statements is true?

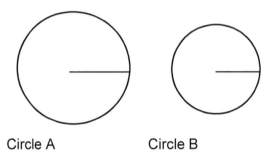

Circle A   Circle B

A) The difference between the areas of the circles is 2.
B) The difference between the areas of the circles is 9π.
C) The difference between the circumferences of the circles is 2.
D) The difference between the circumferences of the circles is 4π.

132) In the standard (*x*, *y*) plane, what is the distance between $\left(4\sqrt{7}, -2\right)$ and $\left(7\sqrt{7}, 4\right)$?

A) $3\sqrt{11}$
B) 27
C) 36
D) 99

133) The graph below illustrates which of the following functions?

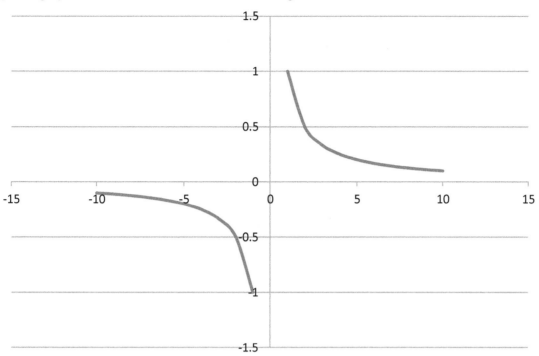

A) $f(x) = \frac{1}{x}$ B) $f(x) = \frac{x}{2}$ C) $f(x) = x^2 + 2$ D) $f(x) = x^2 - 2$

134) Tables of vales are given below for $f_1(x)$ and $f_2(x)$. Find the value of $f_2(f_1(2))$.

x	$f_1(x)$
1	3
2	5
3	7
4	9
5	11

x	$f_2(x)$
2	4
3	9
4	16
5	25
6	36

A) 4   B) 5

C) 9   D) 25

135) x and y are integers. If $f_1(x) = x^2$, which of the values for x below has the smallest value for $f_1(x)$?

A) –5   B) –6   C) 0   D) 5

136) According to the graph, the two highest categories accounted for what percentage of use in total?

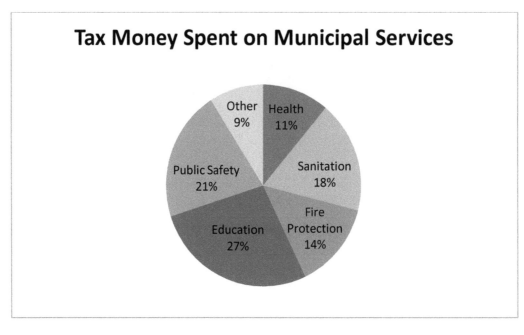

A)   32%   B) 41%   C) 48%   D) 52%

137) The students at Lyndon High School have been asked about their plans to attend the Homecoming Dance. The chart below shows the responses of each grade level by percentages. Which figure below best approximates the percentage of the total number of students from all four grades who will attend the dance? Note that each grade level has roughly the same number of students.

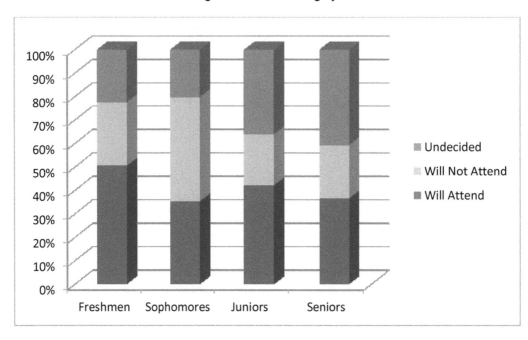

A)   25%   B) 35%   C) 45%   D) 55%

138) The pictograph below illustrates the results of a customer satisfaction survey by region. Each of the four regions has one salesperson. Salespeople in each region receive bonuses based on the amount of positive customer feedback they receive. If the salespeople from all four regions received $540 in bonuses in total, how much bonus money does the company pay each individual salesperson per satisfied customer?

Region 1	
Region 2	
Region 3	
Region 4	

Each represents positive feedback from 10 customers.

A) $4.00
B) $4.50
C) $4.90
D) $5.00

139) A dance judge awards a number from 1 to 10 to score dancers during a TV show. During one show, he judged five dancers and awarded the following scores: 9.9, 9.9, 8.2, 7.6 and 6.8. What was the median value of his scores for this show?

A)   8.2   B) 8.48   C) 9.9   D) 3.1

140) Find the standard deviation for the following scores on a quiz, which has a maximum score of 150: 150, 149, 124, 103, and 99.

A) 223,162   B) 472.4   C) 25   D) 21.73

141) Four members of a family are having a meal in a restaurant. They each have a main dish and a desert. The main dishes are all the same price each, and the deserts are also all the same price for each dessert. The main dishes cost $8 each. The total cost of their meal is $48. How much did each of their deserts cost?

A) $3.75   B) $4   C) $6   D) $22

142) If $\ominus$ is a special operation defined by $(x \ominus y) = (5x + 2y)$ and $(6 \ominus z) = 44$, then $z = ?$

A)   32   B) 36   C) 7   D) 17

143) Express as a logarithmic function: $6^3 = 216$

A) $6 = \log_3 32$ B) $3 = \log_6 216$ C) $6 = \log_{216} 3$ D) $216 = \log_6 3$

144) Retail prices for a particular item at four different stores are provided below. Calculate the variance in the retail prices: $12; $14; $10; $8

A) $5　　　　　　　　B) $6　　　　　　　　C) $9　　　　　　　　D) $2.24

145) A bag contains 5 red balloons, 10 orange balloons, 8 green balloons, and 12 purple balloons. If a balloon is drawn from the bag at random, what is the probability that it will be orange?

A) $\frac{2}{7}$　　　　　　B) $\frac{1}{4}$　　　　　　C) $\frac{1}{10}$　　　　　　D) $\frac{1}{35}$

146) A deck of cards contains 13 hearts, 13 diamonds, 13 clubs, and 13 spades. Cards are selected from the deck at random. Once selected, the cards are discarded and are not placed back into the deck. Two spades, one heart, and a club are drawn from the deck. What is the probability that the next card drawn from the deck will be a heart?

A) $^1/_{13}$　　　　　　B) $^1/_{12}$　　　　　　C) $^{13}/_{52}$　　　　　　D) $^1/_4$

147) The term BPM, heartbeats per minute, measures how many heartbeats a person has every 60 seconds. To calculate BPM, the heartbeat is taken for ten seconds, represented by variable B. What equation is used to calculate BPM?

A) BPM ÷ 60　　　B) BPM ÷ 10　　　C) B6　　　　　　D) B10

148) The ideal BPM of a healthy person is 60. What equation is used to calculate by how much a person's BPM exceeds the ideal BPM?

A) 60 + BPM　　　B) 60 – BPM　　　C) BPM + 60　　　D) BPM – 60

149) Shawn's final grade for a class is based on his grades from two projects, X and Y. Project X counts toward 45% of his final grade. Project Y counts toward 55% of his final grade. What equation can be used to calculate Shawn's final grade for this class?

A) .55X + .45Y　　　B) .45X + .55Y　　　C) (.45X + .55Y) ÷ 2　　　D) X + Y

150) The number of visitors a museum had on Tuesday (T) was twice as much as the number of visitors it had on Monday (M). The number of visitors it had on Wednesday (W) was 20% greater than that on Tuesday. Which equation can be used to calculate the total number of visitors to the museum for the three days?

A) M + 2T + W　　　B) M + 1.2T + W　　　C) W +.20W + 2T + M　　　D) 5.4M

151) Solve for x: $x^2 + 4x + 3 > 0$
A) $x < -3$ or $x > -1$ B) $x < -3$ or $x < -1$
C) $x > -3$ or $x < -1$ D) $x > -3$ or $x > -1$

152) $(x - 9y)^2 = ?$
A) $x^2 + 81y^2$ B) $x^2 - 18xy - 18y^2$ C) $x^2 - 18xy + 81y^2$ D) $x^2 + 18xy - 81y^2$

153) $6 + \dfrac{x}{4} \geq 22$, then $x \geq$?
A) -8 B) 64 C) -64 D) 128

154) $(x^2 - x - 12) \div (x - 4) = ?$
A) $(x + 3)$ B) $(x - 3)$ C) $(-x + 3)$ D) $(-x - 3)$

155) Factor using the greatest common factor: $18xy - 24x^2y - 48y^2x^2$
A) $6xy(3 - 4x - 8xy)$ B) $3xy(6 - 8x - 16xy)$
C) $6x^2y(3 - 4 - 8y)$ D) $6xy(3 - 4x + 8xy)$

156) $\sqrt{15x^3} \times \sqrt{8x^2}$

A) $\sqrt{23x^5}$ B) $2x^2\sqrt{30x^3}$ C) $2x^2\sqrt{30x}$ D) $\sqrt{23x^6}$

157) Which one of the following is a solution to the following ordered pairs of equations?
    $-3x - 1 = y$
    $x + 7 = y$
A) $(5, -2)$ B) $(-2, 5)$ C) $(2, 5)$ D) $(5, 2)$

158) $x^{-4} = ?$
A) $4\sqrt{x}$ B) $\sqrt[-4]{x}$ C) $x^4 \div 1$ D) $1 \div x^4$

159) If $5(4\sqrt{x} - 8) = 40$, then $x = ?$

A) $\dfrac{5}{12}$ B) 4 C) 16 D) $\sqrt{\dfrac{5}{12}}$

160) $\sqrt[3]{\dfrac{8}{27}} = ?$

A) $\dfrac{2}{3}$ B) $\dfrac{4}{9}$ C) $\dfrac{2}{9}$ D) $\dfrac{\sqrt{8}}{9}$

161) For all $a \neq b$, $\dfrac{5a/b}{2a/(a-b)} = ?$

A) $\dfrac{10a^2}{ab - b^2}$ B) $\dfrac{a - b}{2b}$ C) $\dfrac{5a - 5b}{2}$ D) $\dfrac{5a - 5b}{2b}$

162) The line on the *xy*-graph below forms the diameter of the circle. What is the area of the circle?

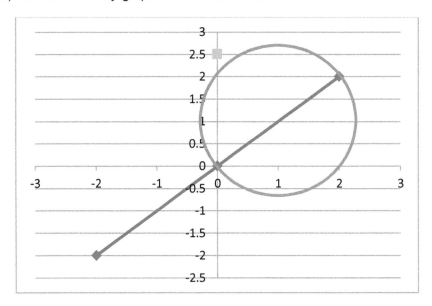

A) π B) 2π C) $\frac{\pi}{2}$ D) 2.5π

163) Which one of the scatterplots below most strongly suggests a negative linear relationship between *x* and *y*?

A)

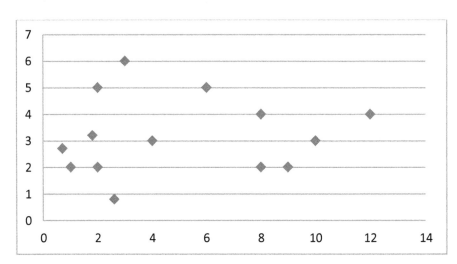

B)

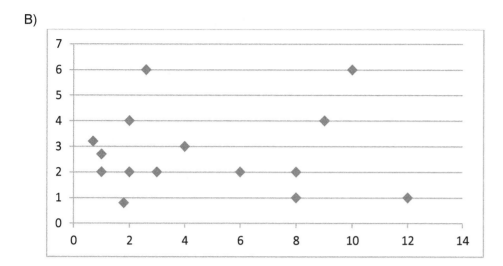

C)

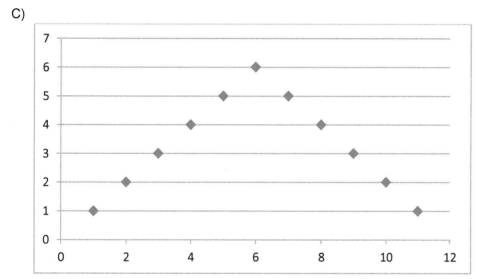

D)

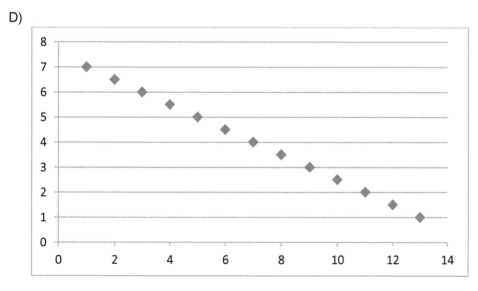

164) An airplane flew at a constant speed, traveling 780 miles in 2 hours. The graph below shows the total miles the airplane traveled in 20 minute intervals. According to the graph, how many miles did the plane travel in the last 40 minutes of its journey?

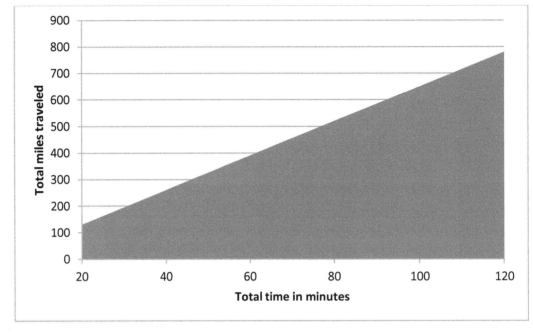

A) 120   B) 180   C) 200   D) 260

165) Find the area of the right triangle that has a base of 4 and a height of 15.

A)   20   B) 30   C) 60   D) 120

166) A small circle has a radius of 5 inches, and a larger circle has a radius of 8 inches. What is the difference in inches between the circumferences of the two circles?
A)   3
B)   6
C) 6π
D) 9π

167) Which of the following statements about isosceles triangles is true?
A)   Isosceles triangles have two equal sides.
B)   When an altitude is drawn in an isosceles triangle, two equilateral triangles are formed.
C)   The base of an isosceles triangle must be shorter than the length of each of the other two sides.
D)   The sum of the measurements of the interior angles of an isosceles triangle must be equal to 360°.

168) The illustration below shows a right circular cone. The entire cone has a base radius of 9 and a height of 18.

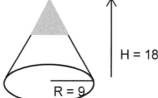

H = 18

R = 9

The shaded portion at the top of the cone has a height of 6. What is the volume of the shaded portion?

A) 18π
B) 36π
C) 48π
D) 486π

169) The diagram below depicts a cell phone tower. The height of the tower from point B at the center of its base to point T at the top is 30 meters, and the distance from point B of the tower to point A on the ground is 18 meters. What is the approximate distance from point A on the ground to the top (T) of the cell phone tower?

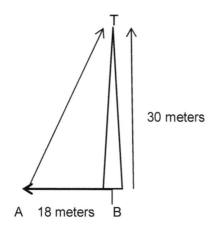

30 meters

A   18 meters   B

A) 10 meters
B) 20 meters
C) 30 meters
D) 35 meters

170) The graph of a line is shown on the *xy* plane below. The point that has the *x*-coordinate of 160 is not shown. What is the corresponding *y*-coordinate of that point?

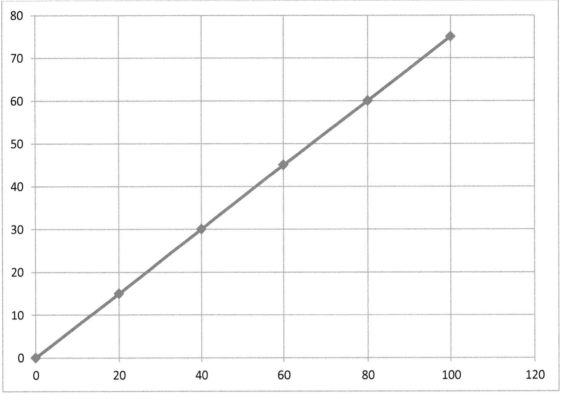

A) 115   B) 120   C) 125   D) 130

171) The central angle in the circle below measures 30° and is subtended by arc *A* which is 7π centimeters in length. How many centimeters long is the radius of this circle?

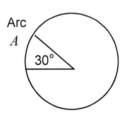

A) 21   B) 42   C) 6π D) 6

172) A company has decided to remodel their offices. They currently have 3 offices that measure 10 feet by 10 feet each and a common area that also measures 10 feet by 10 feet. When the offices are remodeled, there will be one large office that will be 20 feet by 10 feet and two small offices that will each be 10 feet by 8 feet. The remaining space is to be allocated to the new common area. What are the dimensions of the new common area?

A) 4 × 10   B) 8 × 10   C) 10 × 10   D) 4 × 8

173) Triangle QRS is a right-angled triangle. Side Q and side R form the right angle, and side S is the hypotenuse. If Q = 3 and R = 2, what is the length of side S?

A) 5   B) $\sqrt{5}$ C) $\sqrt{13}$ D) 13

174) Liz wants to put new vinyl flooring in her kitchen. She will buy the flooring in square pieces that measure 1 square foot each. The entire room is 8 feet by 12 feet. The cupboards are two feet deep from front to back. Flooring will not be put under the cupboards. A diagram of her kitchen is provided.

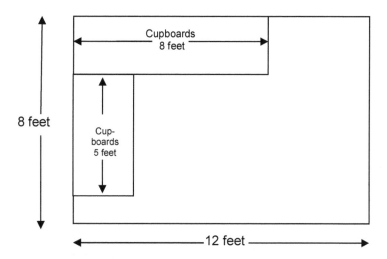

How many pieces of vinyl will Liz need to cover her floor?

A) 120   B) 96   C) 70   D) 84

175) The diagram below shows a figure made from a semicircle, a rectangle, and an equilateral triangle. The rectangle has a length of 18 inches and a width of 10 inches. What is the perimeter of the figure?

A) 56 inches + 5π inches   B) 56 inches + 10π inches
C) 56 inches + 12.5π inches   D) 56 inches + 25π inches

176) The illustration below shows a pyramid with a base width of 3, a base length of 5, and a volume of 30. What is the height of the pyramid?

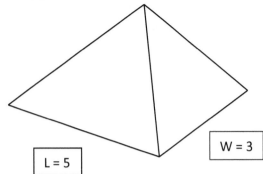

L = 5

W = 3

A) 2   B) 3   C) 5   D) 6

177) Find the x and y intercepts of the following equation: $5x^2 + 4y^2 = 120$

A) $(0, \sqrt{30})$ and $(\sqrt{24}, 0)$

B) $(0, 30)$ and $(24, 0)$

C) $(\sqrt{24}, 0)$ and $(0, \sqrt{30})$

D) $(30, 0)$ and $(0, 24)$

178) Consider a two-dimensional linear graph where $x = 4$ and $y = 15$. The line crosses the y axis at 3. What is the slope of this line?

A) $\frac{1}{15}$ B) 3   C) $-\frac{1}{3}$ D) –3

179) The perimeter of a rectangle is 48 meters. If the width were doubled and the length were increased by 5 meters, the perimeter would be 92 meters. What are the length (L) and width (W) of the original rectangle?

A)   W = 17, L = 7   B) W = 7, L = 17   C) W = 34, L = 14   D) W = 24, L = 46

180) $4 = \log_4 256$ is equivalent to which of the following?

A) 4^4 B)   8   C) $4\sqrt{256}$ D) $\frac{256}{4}$

181) The graph below illustrates which of the following functions?

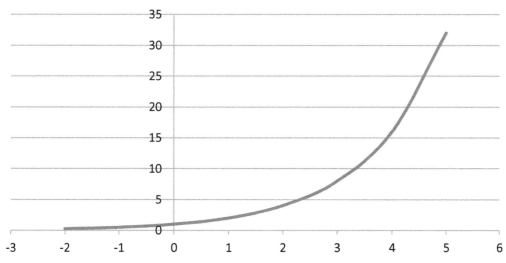

A) $f(x) = \frac{1}{x}$　　　B) $f(x) = 2^x$　　　C) $f(x) = \sqrt{x}$　　　D) $f(x) = x^2$

182) Express 7^3 as a logarithmic function.

A) $343 = \log_7 3$　　　B) $343 = \log_3 7$　　　C) $7 = \log_3 343$　　　D) $3 = \log_7 343$

183) If $f_1(x) = x^2 + x$, what is the value of $f_1(5)$?

A) 5　　　　　B) 10　　　　　C) 25　　　　　D) 30

184) The chart below shows data on the number of vehicles involved in accidents in Cedar Valley. Pick-ups and vans were involved in approximately what percentage of total vehicle accidents on June 1?

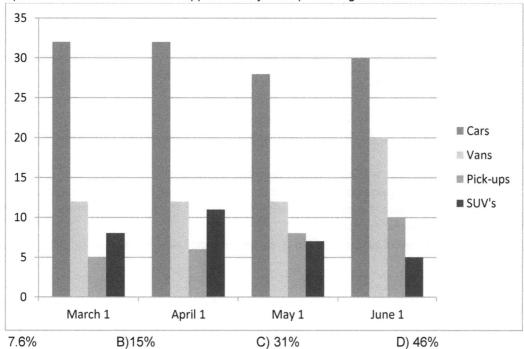

A)   7.6%　　　　　B)15%　　　　　C) 31%　　　　　D) 46%

185) The pictograph below shows the number of traffic violations that occur every week in a certain city. The fine for speeding violations is $50 per violation. The fine for other violations is $20 per violation. The total collected for all three types of violations was $6,000. What is the fine for each parking violation?

Speeding	☆ ☆
Parking	☆
Other violations	☆ ☆ ☆

Each ☆ represents 30 violations.

A) $20   B) $30   C) $40   D) $100

186) The graph below shows the relationship between the number of days of rain per month and the amount of people who exercise outdoors per month. What relationship can be observed?

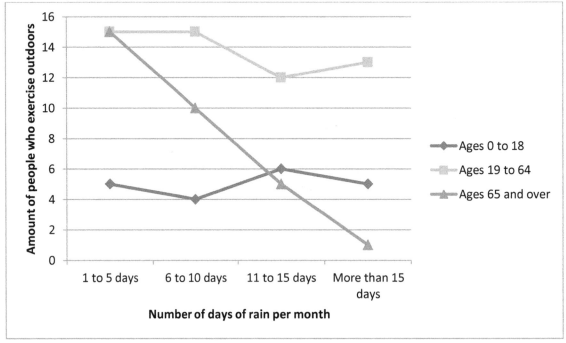

A) Young children are reliant upon an adult in order to exercise outdoors.

B) The exercise habits of working age people seem to fluctuate proportionately to the amount of rainfall.

C) In the 19 to 64 age group, there is a negative relationship between the number of days of rain and the amount of people who exercise outdoors.

D) People aged 65 and over seem less inclined to exercise outdoors when there is more rain.

187) The radius of a circle is 16 and the radians of the subtended angle measure $^3\pi/_4$. What is the length of the arc subtending the central angle?

A) 3π B) 4π C) 12π D) 16π

188) Seven members of a support group are trying to gain weight. So far, the weight gain in kilograms for each of the seven members of the group is: 12, 15, 3, 7, 21, 14, and 12. What is the range of the amount of weight gain for this support group?

A)   18   B) 12   C) 14   D) 7

189) Looking at our seven group members from question 188 above, what is the mode?

A)   18   B) 12   C) 14   D) 7

190) The price of widgets is $2 each and the price of whatsits is $25 each. Zafira bought widgets and whatsits in one transaction, and she paid $85 in total. If she bought 3 whatsits, how many widgets did she buy?

A) 2   B) 3   C) 5   D) 8

191) Find the median of the following data set: 10, 12, 8, 2, 5, 21, 8, 6, 2, 3

A) 7   B) 6.5   C) 2   D) 19

192) The median and mean of 9 numbers are 8 and 9 respectively. The 9 numbers are positive integers greater than zero. If each of the 9 numbers is increased by 2, which of the following must be true of the increased numbers?

A)   The mean will be greater than before, but the median will remain the same.
B)   The median will be greater than before, but the mean will remain the same.
C)   Both the median and mean will be greater than before.
D)   The median and mean will be the same as before, but the range will increase.

193) A entertainer pulls colored ribbons out of a box at random for a dance routine. The box contains 5 red ribbons and 6 blue ribbons. The other ribbons in the box are green. If a ribbon is pulled out of the box at random, the probability that the ribbon is red is $^1/_3$. How many green ribbons are in the box?

A) 3   B) 4   C) 5   D) 6

194) A participant in a 100 mile endurance event ran at a speed of 5 miles per hour for the first 80 miles of the event and x miles per hour for the last 20 miles of the event. What equation represents the participant's average speed for the entire event?

A) $100 \div [(80 \div 5) + (20 \div x)]$ B) $100 \times [(80 \div 5) + (20 \div x)]$
C) $100 \div [(80 \times 5) + (20 \times x)]$ D) $100 \times [(80 \times 5) + (20 \times x)]$

195) Which of these numbers could be a probability?

A) -0.02   B) $^8/_5$ C) 1.002   D) $^1/_4$

196) A driver travels at 60 miles per hour for two and a half hours before her car fails to start at a service station. She has to wait two hours while the car is repaired before she can continue driving. She then drives at 75 miles an hour for the remainder of her journey. She is traveling to her mother's house, and her journey is 240 miles in total. If she left home at 6:00 am, what time will she arrive at her mother's house?

A)   9:30 am
B)   11:30 am
C)   11:42 am
D)   11:50 am

197) A clothing store sells jackets and jeans at a discount during a sales period. T represents the number of jackets sold and N represents the number of jeans sold. The total amount of money the store collected for sales of jeans and jackets during the sales period was $4,000. The amount of money earned from selling jackets was one-third of that earned from selling jeans. The jeans sold for $20 a pair. How many pairs of jeans did the store sell during the sales period?

A)   15
B)   20
C)   150
D)   200

198) Which of the following steps will solve the equation for x: $18 = 3(x + 5)$
A)   Subtract 5 from each side of the equation, and then divide both sides by 3.
B)   Subtract 18 from each side of the equation, and then divide both sides by 5.
C)   Multiply both x and 5 by 3 on the right side of the equation. Then subtract 15 from each side of the equation.
D)   Divide each side of the equation by 3. Then subtract 5 from both sides of the equation.

199) The number of bottles of soda that a soft drink factory can produce during D number of days using production method A is represented by the equation: $D^5 + 12,000$. Alternatively, the number of bottles of soda that can be produced using method B is represented by this equation: $D \times 10,000$. What is the largest number of bottles of soda that can be produced by the factory during a 10 day period?

A)   10,000
B)   12,000
C)   100,000
D)   112,000

200) An athlete ran 10 miles in 1.5 hours. The graph below shows the miles the athlete ran every 10 minutes. According to the graph, how many miles did the athlete run in the first 30 minutes?

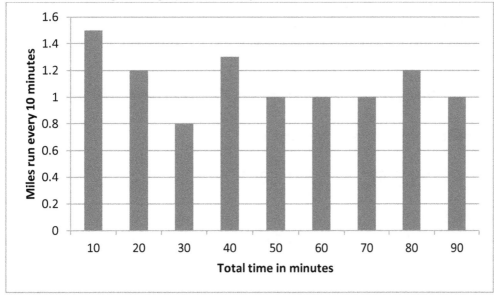

A) 0.8 miles   B) 2.0 miles   C) 3.0 miles   D) 3.5 miles

TSI Math Practice Test Set 5 – Questions 201 to 250

201) Perform the operations: $(5x - 2)(3x^2 + 5x - 8)$

A) $15x^3 + 19 + 50x + 16$

B) $15x^3 + 19x^2 + 70x - 16$

C) $15x^3 + 19x^2 - 50x + 16$

D) $15x^3 + 19x^2 - 70x + 16$

202) Solve for x and y: $x + 5y = 24$ and $8x + 2y = 40$

A) (4, 4) B) (–4, 4) C) (40, 4) D) (4, 38)

203) Perform the operation and express as one fraction: $\dfrac{2}{10x} + \dfrac{3}{12x^2}$

A) $\dfrac{30x}{24x^2}$

B) $\dfrac{5}{10x + 12x^2}$

C) $\dfrac{4x + 5}{20x^2}$

D) $\dfrac{24x^2}{30x}$

204) $\sqrt{50} + 4\sqrt{32} + 7\sqrt{2}$ = ?

A) $8\sqrt{58}$ B) $28\sqrt{2}$ C) $15\sqrt{58}$ D) $16\sqrt{2}$

205) $10a^2b^3c \div 2ab^2c^2$ = ?

A) $5c \div ab$ B) $5a \div bc$ C) $5ab \div c$ D) $5ac \div b$

206) $\dfrac{\sqrt{48}}{3} + \dfrac{5\sqrt{5}}{6}$ = ?

A) $\dfrac{4\sqrt{3} + 5\sqrt{5}}{6}$

B) $\dfrac{8\sqrt{3} + 5\sqrt{5}}{6}$

C) $\dfrac{\sqrt{48} + 5\sqrt{5}}{9}$

D) $\dfrac{6\sqrt{48} + 5\sqrt{5}}{18}$

207) What is the value of $\dfrac{x-3}{2-x}$ when $x = 1$?

A) 2 B) –2 C) $^1/_2$ D) $-^1/_2$

208) $\sqrt[3]{5} \times \sqrt[3]{7}$ = ?

A) $\sqrt[3]{13}$ B) $\sqrt[6]{13}$ C) $\sqrt[9]{13}$ D) $\sqrt[3]{35}$

209) If x and y are positive integers, the expression $\dfrac{1}{\sqrt{x} - \sqrt{y}}$ is equivalent to which of the following?

A) $\sqrt{x} - y$ B) $\sqrt{x} + y$ C) $\dfrac{\sqrt{x} - y}{1}$ D) $\dfrac{\sqrt{x} + \sqrt{y}}{x - y}$

210) If $x + y = 5$ and $a + b = 4$, what is the value of $(3x + 3y)(5a + 5b)$?

A) 9 B) 35 C) 200 D) 300

211) What are two possible values of x for the following equation? $x^2 + 6x + 8 = 0$

A) 1 and 2 B) 2 and 4 C) 6 and 8 D) –2 and –4

212) Which of the following mathematical expressions equals $^3/_{xy}$?

A) $^3/_x \times ^3/_y$ B) $3 \div 3xy$ C) $3 \div (xy)$ D) $^1/_3 \div 3xy$

213) If $\frac{1}{5}x + 3 = 5$, then $x = ?$

A) $\frac{8}{5}$ B) $-\frac{8}{5}$ C) 8 D) 10

214) Solve for x: $x^2 - 12x + 35 < 0$

A) $5 > x > 7$ B) $5 > x$ or $x < 7$
C) $5 < x < 7$ D) $5 < x$ or $x > 7$

215) Factor the following: $2xy - 8x^2y + 6y^2x^2$

A) $2(xy - 4x^2y + 3x^2y^2)$ B) $2xy(-4x + 3xy)$
C) $2xy(1 - 4x + 3xy)$ D) $2xy(1 + 4x - 3xy)$

216) Look at the scatterplot below and then choose the best answer from the options that follow.

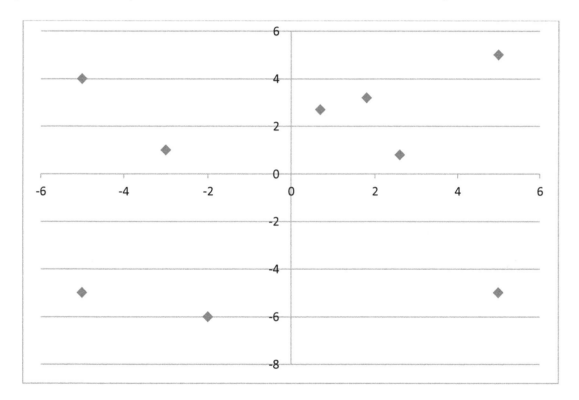

A) The scatterplot suggests a strong positive linear relationship between x and y.
B) The scatterplot suggests a strong negative linear relationship between x and y.
C) The scatterplot suggests a weak positive linear relationship between x and y.
D) The scatterplot suggests that there is no relationship between x and y.

217) The line on the *xy*-graph below forms the diameter of the circle. What is the approximate circumference of the circle?

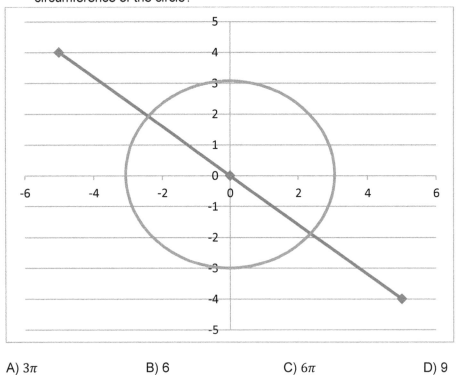

A) 3π B) 6   C) 6π D) 9

218) Mr. Lee is going to build a new garage. The garage will have a square base and a pyramid-shaped roof. The base measurement of the garage is 20 feet. The height of the interior of the garage is 18 feet. The height of the roof from the center of its base to its peak is 15 feet. A diagram of the garage is shown below:

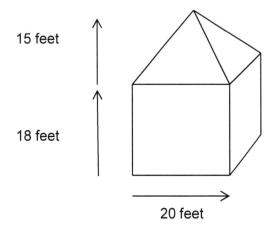

15 feet

18 feet

20 feet

What fraction expresses the ratio of the volume of the roof of the garage to the volume of the base of the garage?

A) $^5/_6$ B) $^5/_{18}$ C) $^1/_4$ D) $^3/_4$

219) A large wheel (L) has a radius of 10 inches. A small wheel (S) has a radius of 6 inches. If the large wheel is going to travel 360 revolutions, how many more revolutions does the small wheel need to make to cover the same distance?

A) 120　　　　　　　B) 240　　　　　　　C) 360　　　　　　　D) 720

220) The vertex of an angle is at the center of a circle. If the angle measures 20 degrees, and the diameter of the circle is 2, what is the arc length relating to the angle?

A) $^{\pi}/_{9}$　　　　　　　B) $^{\pi}/_{18}$　　　　　　　C) 9π　　　　　　　D) 18π

221) A farmer has a rectangular pen in which he keeps animals. He has decided to divide the pen into two parts. To divide the pen, he will erect a fence diagonally from the two corners, as shown in the diagram below. How long in yards is the diagonal fence?

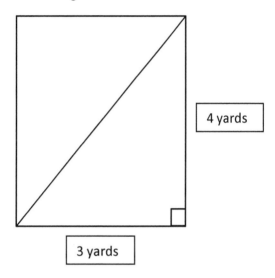

4 yards

3 yards

A) 4　　　　　　　B) 5　　　　　　　C) 5.5　　　　　　　D) 6

222) What is the area of the figure below?

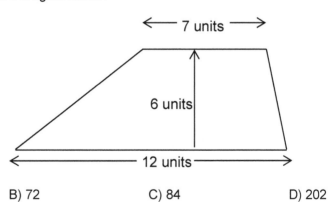

7 units

6 units

12 units

A) 57　　　　　　　B) 72　　　　　　　C) 84　　　　　　　D) 202

223) The illustration below shows a pentagon. The shaded part at the top of the pentagon has a height of 6 inches.

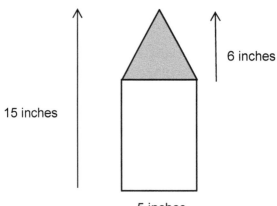

15 inches

6 inches

5 inches

The height of the entire pentagon is 15 inches, and the base of the pentagon is 5 inches. What is the area of the entire pentagon?

A)   15 B) 30 C) 45 D) 60

224) What equation can be used for the radian in a 90° angle?

A) $\pi \times radian \times 2$ B) $\pi \times radian \times 4$ C) $(\pi \div 2) \times radian$ D) $(\pi \times 2) \div radian$

225) The area of a square is 64 square units. This square is made up of smaller squares that measure 4 square units each. How many of the smaller squares are needed to make up the larger square?

A)   8 B) 12 C) 16 D) 24

226) Which of the following statements about parallelograms is true?
A)   A parallelogram has no right angles.
B)   A parallelogram has opposite angles which are congruent.
C)   The opposite sides of a parallelogram are unequal in measure.
D)   A rectangle is not a parallelogram.

227) Which of the following statements best describes supplementary angles?
A)   Supplementary angles must add up to 90 degrees.
B)   Supplementary angles must add up to 180 degrees.
C)   Supplementary angles must add up to 360 degrees.
D)   Supplementary angles must be congruent angles.

228) A is 3 times B, and B is 3 more than 6 times C. Which of the following describes the relationship between A and C?
A)   A is 9 more than 18 times C. B) A is 3 more than 3 times C.
C)   A is 3 more than 18 times C. C) A is 6 more than 3 times C.

229) The graph below illustrates which of the following functions?

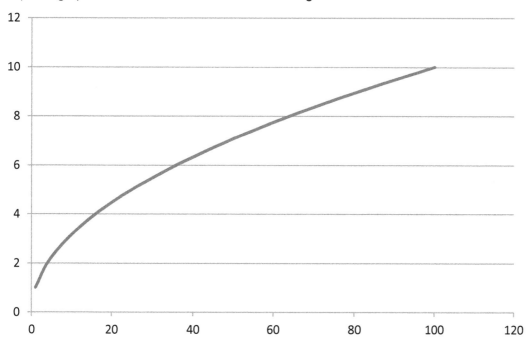

A) $f(x) = \frac{1}{x}$ B) $f(x) = 2^x$ C) $f(x) = \sqrt{x}$ D) $f(x) = x^2$

230) $2 = \log_8 64$ is equivalent to which of the following?

A) 2^8 B) $\sqrt{64}$ C) 8^2 D) 64^2

231) Express 81 as a logarithmic function.
A) $81 = \log_2 9$
B) $2 = \log_9 81$
C) $9 = \log_2 81$
D) $81 = \log_9 2$

232) If $f_2(x) = \sqrt{x} + 3$ and $f_1(x) = 3x + 1$, what is the value of $f_1(f_2(9))$?
A) $\sqrt{28} + 3$
B) 19
C) 28
D) 6

233) The residents of Hendersonville took a census. As part of the census, each resident had to indicate how many relatives they had living within a ten-mile radius of the town. The results of that particular question on the census are represented in the graph below.

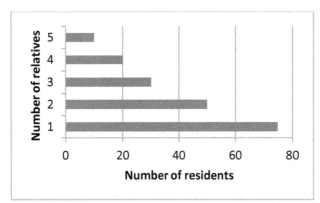

How many residents of Hendersonville had more than 3 relatives living within a ten-mile radius of the town?
A)   10
B)   20
C)   30
D) 155

234) An illusionist has a box of pieces of colored rope for an illusion that he performs at a live show. The box contains 4 pieces of blue rope, 2 pieces of white rope, 1 piece of green rope, 4 pieces of yellow rope, and 5 pieces of black rope. The illusionist selects pieces of rope at random and the first piece of rope he selects is blue. Pieces of rope are not put back in the box once they are selected. What is the probability that he will select a piece of blue rope again on the second draw?

A) $^1/_5$ B) $^1/_4$ C) $^3/_{16}$ D) $^4/_{15}$

235) Mr. Rodriguez teaches a class of 25 students. Ten of the students in his class participate in drama club. In which graph below does the dark gray area represent the percentage of students who participate in drama club?

A)

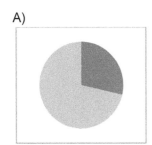

B)

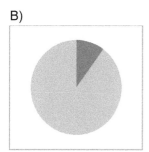

C)

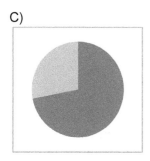

D)

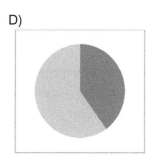

236) The graph below shows the relationship between the total number of hamburgers a restaurant sells and the total sales in dollars for the hamburgers. What is the sales price per hamburger?

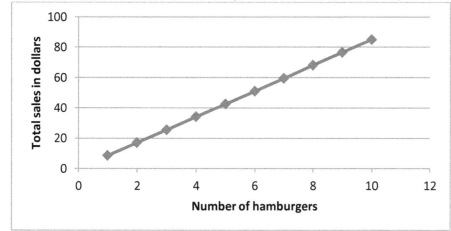

A) $4.00

B) $8.00

C) $8.50

D) $9.50

237) Find the midpoint between the following coordinates: (5, 7) and (11, −3)

A) (2, 5) B) (5, 2) C) (2, 8) D) (8, 2)

238) If $\sqrt{9z + 18} = 9$, then z = ?

A) −1 B) 6 C) 7 D) 63

239) If $z = \dfrac{x}{1-y}$, then y = ?

A) $\dfrac{z}{x}$ B) $\dfrac{x}{z} - 1$ C) $-\dfrac{x}{z} + 1$ D) $z - zx$

240) Perform the operation: $\sqrt{6} \cdot \left(\sqrt{40} + \sqrt{6}\right)$

A) $\sqrt{240} + \sqrt{6}$ B) $\sqrt{46} + 6$ C) 46 D) $4\sqrt{15} + 6$

241) Which of the following is equivalent to $a^{\frac{1}{2}}b^{\frac{1}{4}}c^{\frac{3}{4}}$?

A) $a^2bc^3 \div 4$ B) $4(a^2bc^3)$ C) $\sqrt{a} \times \sqrt[4]{b} \times \sqrt[4]{c^3}$ D) $(ab^{\frac{1}{4}}c^{\frac{3}{4}} \div 2)$

242) $ab^8 \div ab^2$ = ?

A) ab^6 B) ab^4 C) a^2b^6 D) b^6

243) In Brown County Elementary School, parents are advised to have their children vaccinated against five childhood diseases. According to the chart below, how many children were vaccinated against at least three diseases?

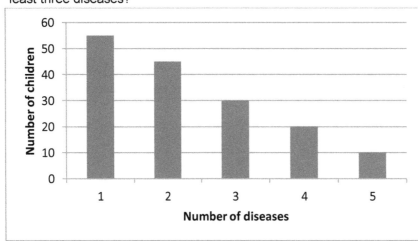

A) 30
B) 50
C) 60
D) 100

244) A doctor measures the pulse for several patients one morning. She recorded these results: 54, 68, 62, 60, 75, 58, 84, and 91. What is the range for this group of patients?

A) 30 B) 37 C) 65 D) 69

245) A wastewater company measures the amount of wastewater usage per household in wastewater units (WWU's). During one calendar quarter, the houses on a particular street had these measurements: 682, 534, 689, 783, and 985. What is the mode of wastewater usage in WWU's for this quarter for these properties?

A) no mode   B) 451   C) 689   D) 734.6

246) 100 participants took an intelligence test. The mean score for the first 50 participants was 82, and the mean score for the next 50 participants was 89. What is the mean test score for all 100 participants?

A) 85.5   B) 86.5   C) 87   D) 88

247) In an trivia contest, the maximum possible amount of points was 50 points per participant. There were six participants in the contest. Their scores were 40, 45, 46, 38, 32, and 49. What was the median score?

A) 17   B) 41.67   C) 42.5   D) 50

248) Perform the operation and express as one fraction: $\dfrac{1}{a+1} + \dfrac{1}{a}$

A) $\dfrac{2}{2a+1}$ B) $\dfrac{a+1}{a}$ C) $\dfrac{a^2+a}{2a+1}$ D) $\dfrac{2a+1}{a^2+a}$

249) For all $x \neq 0$ and $y \neq 0$, $\dfrac{5x}{1/xy} = ?$

A) $\dfrac{5x}{xy}$ B) $\dfrac{xy}{5x}$ C) $\dfrac{5}{y}$ D) $5x^2y$

250) The speed of a rocket is 25,000 miles per hour. How far does the rocket travel in 108,000 seconds?

A) 7.5×10^4 miles   B) 7.5×10^5 miles   C) 7.5×10^6 miles   D) 4.2×10^6 miles

Solutions and Explanations for Practice Test Set 1 – Questions 1 to 50

1) The correct answer is D. The factors of 50 are: 1 × 50 = 50; 2 × 25 = 50; 5 × 10 = 50. If any of your factors are perfect squares, you can simplify the radical. 25 is a perfect square, so, you need to factor inside the radical sign as shown to solve the problem: $\sqrt{50} = \sqrt{25 \times 2} = \sqrt{5^2 \times 2} = \sqrt{5^2} \times \sqrt{2} = 5\sqrt{2}$

2) The correct answer is D. 36 is the common factor, So, factor the amounts inside the radicals and simplify: $\sqrt{36} + 4\sqrt{72} - 2\sqrt{144} = \sqrt{36} + 4\sqrt{36 \times 2} - 2\sqrt{36 \times 4} =$
$\sqrt{6 \times 6} + 4\sqrt{(6 \times 6) \times 2} - 2\sqrt{(6 \times 6) \times 4} = 6 + (4 \times 6)\sqrt{2} - (2 \times 6)\sqrt{4} =$
$6 + 24\sqrt{2} - (12 \times 2) = 6 + 24\sqrt{2} - 24 = -18 + 24\sqrt{2}$

3) The correct answer is A. $\sqrt{7} \times \sqrt{11} = \sqrt{7 \times 11} = \sqrt{77}$

4) The correct answer is B. The cube root is the number which satisfies the equation when multiplied by itself two times: $\sqrt[3]{\dfrac{216}{27}} = \sqrt[3]{\dfrac{6 \times 6 \times 6}{3 \times 3 \times 3}} = \dfrac{6}{3} = 2$

5) The correct answer is A. The base number is 7. Add the exponents: $7^5 \times 7^3 = 7^{(5+3)} = 7^8$

6) The correct answer is B. The base is xy. Subtract the exponents: $xy^6 \div xy^3 = xy^{(6-3)} = xy^3$

7) The correct answer is B. We have the base number of 10 and we are multiplying, so we can add the exponent of 5 to the exponent of −1: (1.7 × 10^5 miles per hour) × (2 × 10^{-1} hours) = 1.7 × 2 × $10^{(5+-1)}$ = 3.4 × 10^4 = 3.4 × 10,000 = 34,000 miles

8) The correct answer is D. When you have a fraction as an exponent, the numerator is new exponent and the denominator goes in front as the root: $\sqrt{x^{\frac{5}{7}}} = \left(\sqrt[7]{x}\right)^5$

9) The correct answer is B. $x^{-5} = \dfrac{1}{x^5}$

10) The correct answer is C. We have a non-zero number raised to the power of zero, so it is equal to 1.

11) The correct answer is C.
$$\dfrac{b + \frac{2}{7}}{\frac{1}{b}} = \left(b + \frac{2}{7}\right) \div \frac{1}{b} = \left(b + \frac{2}{7}\right) \times \frac{b}{1} = b\left(b + \frac{2}{7}\right) = b^2 + \frac{2b}{7}$$

12) The correct answer is D. Find the lowest common denominator for the second fraction. Then add the numerators.
$$\dfrac{x^2}{x^2 + 2x} + \dfrac{8}{x} = \dfrac{x^2}{x^2 + 2x} + \left(\dfrac{8}{x} \times \dfrac{x+2}{x+2}\right) = \dfrac{x^2}{x^2 + 2x} + \dfrac{8x + 16}{x^2 + 2x} = \dfrac{x^2 + 8x + 16}{x^2 + 2x}$$

13) The correct answer is A. Multiply as shown: $\dfrac{2a^3}{7} \times \dfrac{3}{a^2} = \dfrac{2a^3 \times 3}{7 \times a^2} = \dfrac{6a^3}{7a^2}$

Then find the greatest common factor and cancel out to simplify: $\dfrac{6a^3}{7a^2} = \dfrac{6a \times a^2}{7 \times a^2} = \dfrac{6a \times \cancel{a^2}}{7 \times \cancel{a^2}} = \dfrac{6a}{7}$

14) The correct answer is B. Invert and multiply.

$\dfrac{8x + 8}{x^4} \div \dfrac{5x + 5}{x^2} = \dfrac{8x + 8}{x^4} \times \dfrac{x^2}{5x+5} = \dfrac{(8x \times x^2) + (8 \times x^2)}{(x^4 \times 5x) + (x^4 \times 5)} = \dfrac{8x^3 + 8x^2}{5x^5 + 5x^4}$

Then factor out (x + 1) from the numerator and denominator and cancel out:

$\dfrac{8x^3 + 8x^2}{5x^5 + 5x^4} = \dfrac{(8x^2 \times x) + (8x^2 \times 1)}{(5x^4 \times x) + (5x^4 \times 1)} = \dfrac{8x^2(x+1)}{5x^4(x+1)} = \dfrac{8x^2\cancel{(x+1)}}{5x^4\cancel{(x+1)}} = \dfrac{8x^2}{5x^4}$

Finally, factor out x^2 and cancel it out: $\dfrac{8x^2}{5x^4} = \dfrac{x^2 \times 8}{x^2 \times 5x^2} = \dfrac{\cancel{x^2} \times 8}{\cancel{x^2} \times 5x^2} = \dfrac{8}{5x^2}$

15) The correct answer is D. Use the FOIL method to expand the polynomial.
FIRST – Multiply the first term from the first set of parentheses by the first term from the second set of parentheses: (**x** + 4y)(**x** + 4y) = x × x = x²
OUTSIDE – Multiply the first term from the first set of parentheses by the second term from the second set of parentheses: (**x** + 4y)(x + **4y**) = x × 4y = 4xy
INSIDE – Multiply the second term from the first set of parentheses by the first term from the second set of parentheses: (x + **4y**)(**x** + 4y) = 4y × x = 4xy
LAST– Multiply the second term from the first set of parentheses by the second term from the second set of parentheses: (x + **4y**)(x + **4y**) = 4y × 4y = 16y²
Finally, we add all of the products together: x² + 4xy + 4xy + 16y² = x² + 8xy + 16y²

16) The correct answer is C. As the quantity of sugar increases, the amount of sleep also increases. A positive linear relationship therefore exists between the two variables. This is represented in chart C since the amount of sleep is greater when the amount of sugar consumed is higher.

17) The correct answer is C. We can see that the line does not begin on exactly on (5, 5), nor does it begin on (5, 9) because the first point is slightly below the horizontal line for y = 5. Therefore, we can rule out answers A and D. If we look at x = 20 on the graph, we can see that y = 18 at this point.
We can express this as the function: $f(x) = x \times 0.9$. Putting in the values of x from chart (C), we get the following: 5 × 0.9 = 4.5; 10 × 0.9 = 9; 15 × 0.9 =13.5; 20 × 0.9 = 18. This is represented in table C.

18) The correct answer is D. If a term or variable is subtracted within the parentheses, you have to keep the negative sign with it when you multiply.
FIRST: (**x** – y)(**x** + y) = x × x = x²
OUTSIDE: (**x** – y)(x + **y**) = x × y = xy
INSIDE: (x – **y**)(**x** + y) = –y × x = –xy
LAST: (x – **y**)(x + **y**) = –y × y = –y²
SOLUTION: x² + xy + – xy – y² = x² – y²
19) The correct answer is A. First, Isolate the whole numbers.

$50 - \dfrac{3x}{5} \geq 41$

$(50 - 50) - \dfrac{3x}{5} \geq 41 - 50$

$-\dfrac{3x}{5} \geq -9$

Then get rid of the denominator on the fraction.

$-\dfrac{3x}{5} \geq -9$

$\left(5 \times -\dfrac{3x}{5}\right) \geq -9 \times 5$

$-3x \geq -9 \times 5$

$-3x \geq -45$

Then isolate the remaining whole numbers.

$-3x \geq -45$

$-3x \div 3 \geq -45 \div 3$

$-x \geq -45 \div 3$

$-x \geq -15$

Then deal with the negative number.

$-x \geq -15$

$-x + 15 \geq -15 + 15$

$-x + 15 \geq 0$

Finally, isolate the unknown variable as a positive number.

$-x + 15 \geq 0$

$-x + x + 15 \geq 0 + x$

$15 \geq x$

$x \leq 15$

20) The correct answer is D. Substitute values as shown: $x - 2 > 5$ and $y = x - 2$, so $y > 5$. If two wizfits are being purchased, we need to solve for $2y$:

$y \times 2 > 5 \times 2$

$2y > 10$

21) The correct answer is B. For quadratic inequality problems like this one, you need to factor the inequality first. The factors of -9 are: -1×9; -3×3; 1×-9. We do not have a term with only the x variable, so we need factors that add up to zero, so factor as shown:

$x^2 - 9 < 0$

$(x + 3)(x - 3) < 0$

Then find values for x by solving each parenthetical for 0.

$(x + 3) = 0$

$(-3 + 3) = 0$

$x = -3$

$(x - 3) = 0$

$(3 - 3) = 0$

$x = 3$

So, $x > -3$ or $x < 3$

You can then check your work to be sure that you have the inequality signs pointing the right way.

Use –2 to check x > –3. Since –2 > –3 is correct, our proof should also be correct:

$x^2 - 9 < 0$

$-2^2 - 9 < 0$

$4 - 9 < 0$

$-5 < 0$ CORRECT

Use 4 to check for x < 3. Since 4 < 3 is incorrect, our proof should also be incorrect.

$x^2 - 9 < 0$

$4^2 - 9 < 0$

$16 - 9 < 0$

$7 < 0$ INCORRECT

Therefore, we have checked that x > –3 or x < 3.

22) The correct answer is D. We know that the products of 12 are: $1 \times 12 = 12$; $2 \times 6 = 12$; $3 \times 4 = 12$. So, add each of the two factors together to solve the first equation: $1 + 12 = 13$; $2 + 6 = 8$; $3 + 4 = 7$. (3, 4) solves both equations, so it is the correct answer.

23) The correct answer is C. The first term of the second equation is x. To eliminate the x variable, we need to multiply the second equation by 3 because the first equation contains 3x.

$x + 2y = 8$

$(3 \times x) + (3 \times 2y) = (3 \times 8)$

$3x + 6y = 24$

Now subtract the new second equation from the original first equation.

$$\begin{aligned} 3x + 3y &= 15 \\ -(3x + 6y &= 24) \\ \hline -3y &= -9 \end{aligned}$$

Then solve for y.

$-3y = -9$

$-3y \div -3 = -9 \div -3$

$y = 3$

Using our original second equation of $x + 2y = 8$, substitute the value of 3 for y to solve for x.

$x + 2y = 8$

$x + (2 \times 3) = 8$

$x + 6 = 8$

$x + 6 - 6 = 8 - 6$

$x = 2$

24) The correct answer is D. Repeat the operation for each number from 3 to 5.

For $x = 3$: $x - 1 = 3 - 1 = 2$

For $x = 4$: $x - 1 = 4 - 1 = 3$

For $x = 5$: $x - 1 = 5 - 1 = 4$

Then add the individual results together to get the answer: $2 + 3 + 4 = 9$

25) The correct answer is A. When we compare the equations, we see that operation Đ is division: the number or variable immediately before Đ is is multiplied by 30; and the number or variable immediately after Đ is multiplied by 9. So, the new equation for (3 Đ y) becomes $(30 \times 3) \div (9 \times y) = 10$

$(30 \times 3) \div (9 \times y) = 10$

$90 \div 9y = 10$

$y = 1$

26) The correct answer is B. $x = \log_y Z$ is the same as $y^x = Z$. So, $2 = \log_8 64$ is the same as $8^2 = 64$. Check your answer by performing the operation on the number with the exponent: $8^2 = 8 \times 8 = 64$

27) The correct answer is C. Deduct the degrees provided for angle A from 180° to find out the total degrees of the two other angles: 180° − 32° = 148°. Since this is an isosceles triangle, the remaining two angles are have the same measurement. So, divide by two in order to find out how many degrees each angle has: 148° ÷ 2 = 74°

28) The correct answer is B. The angle given in the problem is 90°. If we divide the total of 360° in the circle by the 90° angle, we have: 360 ÷ 90 = 4. You can think of arc length as the partial circumference of a circle, so we can visualize that there are 4 such arcs along this circle. We can then multiply the number of arcs by the length of each arc to get the circumference of the circle: $4 \times 8\pi = 32\pi$ (circumference). Finally, use the formula for the circumference of the circle to solve.

Circumference = $\pi \times$ radius $\times$ 2

$32\pi = \pi \times 2 \times$ radius

$32\pi \div 2 = \pi \times 2 \times$ radius $\div 2$

$16\pi = \pi \times$ radius

$16 =$ radius

29) The correct answer is D. The area of a rectangle is equal to its length times its width. The field is 32 yards wide and 100 yards long, so now we can substitute the values.

rectangle area = width × length

rectangle area = 32 × 100

rectangle area = 3200

30) The correct answer is A. Substitute the value of the diameter into the formula:

circumference = D × π = 6π

31) The correct answer is D. The center of this circle is (−5, 5) and the point of tangency is (−5, 0). We need to subtract these two coordinates in order to find the length of the radius: (−5, 5) − (−5, 0) = (0, 5) In other words, the radius length is 5, so the diameter length is 10.

32) The correct answer is C. The base length of the triangle described in the problem, which is line segment YZ, is not given. So, we need to calculate the base length using the Pythagorean theorem. According to the Pythagorean theorem, the length of the hypotenuse is equal to the square root of the sum of the squares of the two other sides.

$\sqrt{A^2 + B^2} = C$

$\sqrt{4^2 + B^2} = 5$

$\sqrt{16 + B^2} = 5$

Now square each side of the equation in order to solve for the base length.

$$\sqrt{16 + B^2} = 5$$
$$\left(\sqrt{16 + B^2}\right)^2 = 5^2$$
$$16 + B^2 = 25$$
$$16 - 16 + B^2 = 25 - 16$$
$$B^2 = 9$$
$$\sqrt{B^2} = \sqrt{9}$$
$$B = 3$$

Now solve for the area of the triangle.

triangle area = (base × height) ÷ 2
triangle area = (3 × 4) ÷ 2
triangle area = 12 ÷ 2
triangle area = 6

33) The correct answer is D. Triangle XYZ is a 30° / 60°/ 90° triangle. Using the Pythagorean theorem, its sides are therefore in the ratio of $1 : \sqrt{3} : 2$. Using relative measurements, the line segment opposite the 30° angle is 1 unit long, the line segment opposite the 60° angle is $\sqrt{3}$ units long, and the line segment opposite the right angle (the hypotenuse) is 2 units long. In this problem, line segment XY is opposite the 30° angle, so it is 1 proportional unit long. Line segment YZ is opposite the 60° angle, so it is $\sqrt{3}$ proportional units long. Line segment XZ (the hypotenuse) is the line opposite the right angle, so it is 2 proportional units long. So, in order to keep the measurements in proportion, we need to set up the following proportion: $\frac{XY}{YZ} = \frac{1}{\sqrt{3}}$. Now substitute the known measurement of YZ from the above figure, which is 5 in this problem.

$$\frac{XY}{YZ} = \frac{1}{\sqrt{3}}$$
$$\frac{XY}{5} = \frac{1}{\sqrt{3}}$$
$$\left(\frac{XY}{5} \times 5\right) = \left(\frac{1}{\sqrt{3}} \times 5\right)$$
$$XY = \frac{5}{\sqrt{3}}$$

34) The correct answer is C. Write out the formula: (length × 2) + (width × 2). Then substitute the values. (17 × 2) + (4 × 2) = 34 + 8 = 42

35) The correct answer is C. A radian is the measurement of an angle at the center of a circle which is subtended by an arc that is equal in length to the radius of the circle. We need to use the formula to calculate the length of the arc: s = r θ. Substitute values to solve the problem.

radius (r) = 4
radians (θ) = $^\pi/_4$
s = r θ
s = 4 × $^\pi/_4$
s = π

36) The correct answer is C. Substitute the values from the problem.

cone volume = [height × radius^2 × π] ÷ 3

cone volume = [9 × 4^2 × π] ÷ 3

cone volume = [9 × 16 × π] ÷ 3

cone volume = 144π ÷ 3

cone volume = 48π

37) The correct answer is B. First, find the midpoint of the x coordinates for (**−4**, 2) and (**8**,−6).

midpoint $x = (x_1 + x_2) \div 2$

midpoint $x = (-4 + 8) \div 2$

midpoint $x = 4 \div 2$

midpoint $x = 2$

Then find the midpoint of the y coordinates for (−4, **2**) and (8,**−6**).

midpoint $y = (y_1 + y_2) \div 2$

midpoint $y = (2 + -6) \div 2$

midpoint $y = -4 \div 2$

midpoint $y = -2$

So, the midpoint is (2, −2)

38) The correct answer is D. Substitute the values provided (2, 3) and (6, 7) into the formula.

$d = \sqrt{(x_2 - x_1)^2 + (y_2 - y_1)^2}$

$d = \sqrt{(6 - 2)^2 + (7 - 3)^2}$

$d = \sqrt{4^2 + 4^2}$

$d = \sqrt{16 + 16}$

$d = \sqrt{32}$

39) The correct answer is A. Substitute the values into the slope-intercept formula.

$y = mx + b$

$315 = m5 + 15$

$315 - 15 = m5 + 15 - 15$

$300 = m5$

$300 \div 5 = m5 \div 5$

$60 = m$

40) The correct answer is A. The x intercept is the point at which a line crosses the x axis of a graph. In order for the line to cross the x axis, y must be equal to zero at that particular point of the graph. On the other hand, the y intercept is the point at which the line crosses the y axis. So, in order for the line to cross the y axis, x must be equal to zero at that particular point of the graph. First, substitute 0 for y in order to find the x intercept.

$x^2 + 2y^2 = 144$

$x^2 + (2 \times 0) = 144$

$x^2 + 0 = 144$

$x^2 = 144$

$x = 12$

Then substitute 0 for x in order to find the y intercept.

$x^2 + 2y^2 = 144$

$(0 \times 0) + 2y^2 = 144$

$0 + 2y^2 = 144$

$2y^2 \div 2 = 144 \div 2$

$y^2 = 72$

$y = \sqrt{72}$

So, the y intercept is (0, $\sqrt{72}$) and the x intercept is (12, 0).

41) The correct answer is A. The outcome of an earlier roll does not affect the outcome of the next roll. When rolling a pair of dice, the possibility of an odd number is always $^1/_2$, just as the possibility of an even number is always $^1/_2$. We can prove this mathematically by looking at the possible outcomes:

1,1 1,2 1,3 1,4 1,5 1,6
2,1 2,2 2,3 2,4 2,5 2,6
3,1 3,2 3,3 3,4 3,5 3,6
4,1 4,2 4,3 4,4 4,5 4,6
5,1 5,2 5,3 5,4 5,5 5,6
6,1 6,2 6,3 6,4 6,5 6,6

The odd number combinations are highlighted:

1,1 **1,2** 1,3 **1,4** 1,5 **1,6**
2,1 2,2 **2,3** 2,4 **2,5** 2,6
3,1 **3,2** 3,3 **3,4** 3,5 **3,6**
4,1 4,2 **4,3** 4,4 **4,5** 4,6
5,1 **5,2** 5,3 **5,4** 5,5 **5,6**
6,1 6,2 **6,3** 6,4 **6,5** 6,6

So, we can see that an odd number will be rolled half of the time.

42) The correct answer is D. To find the mean, add up all of the items in the set and then divide by the number of items in the set. Here we have 7 numbers in the set, so we get our answer as follows:
(89 + 65 + 75 + 68 + 82 + 74 + 86) ÷ 7 = 539 ÷ 7 = 77

43) The correct answer is A. The mode is the number that occurs the most frequently in the set. Our data set is: 1, 1, 3, 2, 4, 3, 1, 2, 1. The number 1 occurs 4 times in the set, which is more frequently than any other number in the set, so the mode is 1.

44) The correct answer is B. The problem provides the number set: 8.19, 7.59, 8.25, 7.35, 9.10
First of all, put the numbers in ascending order: 7.35, 7.59, 8.19, 8.25, 9.10. Then find the one that is in the middle: 7.35, 7.59, **8.19**, 8.25, 9.10

45) The correct answer is C. To calculate the range, the low number in the set is deducted from the high number in the set. The problem set is: 98.5, 85.5, 80.0, 97, 93, 92.5, 93, 87, 88, 82. The high number is 98.5 and the low number is 80, so the range is 18.5: 98.5 − 80 = 18.5

46) The correct answer is B.
Step 1 – Calculate the arithmetic mean for the data set.
99 + 98 + 74 + 69 + 87 + 83 = 510 total for all six students
510 divided by 6 students equals an arithmetic mean of 85 for the group.

Step 2 – Find the "difference from the mean" for each item in the data set by subtracting the mean from each value.
Student 1: 99 – 85 = 14
Student 2: 98 – 85 = 13
Student 3: 74 – 85 = –11
Student 4: 69 – 85 = –16
Student 5: 87 – 85 = 2
Student 6: 83 – 85 = –2

Step 3 – Square the "difference from the mean" for each item in the data set.

Student 1: 14^2 = 196
Student 2: 13^2 = 169
Student 3: $–11^2$ = 121
Student 4: $–16^2$ = 256
Student 5: 2^2 = 4
Student 6: $–2^2$ = 4

Step 4 – Calculate the mean of the squared figures to calculate the variance.

Variance = 196 + 169 + 121 + 256 + 4 + 4 = 750 ÷ 6 = 125

47) The correct answer is C. The standard deviation of a data set measures the spread of the data around the mean of the data set. The standard deviation is calculated by taking the square root of the variance. So, we use the variance of 125 calculated in the previous question:
The square root is $\sqrt{125} = \sqrt{5 \times 5 \times 5} = 5\sqrt{5}$

48) The correct answer is A. Divide the number of observations less than x by the total number of observations and then multiply by 100. First find out how many students had scores less than 90: 32 – 8 = 24. Then divide: 24 ÷ 32 = 0.75. Then multiply by 100: 0.75 × 100 = 75. If a student had a score of 91 or more, he or she was in the 75th percentile.

49) The correct answer is C. At the beginning of the year, 15% of the 1,500 creatures were fish, so there were 225 fish at the beginning of the year (1,500 × 0.15 = 225). In order to find the percentage of fish at the end of the year, we first need to add up the percentages for the other animals: 40% + 23% + 21% = 84%. Then subtract this amount from 100% to get the remaining percentage for the fish: 100% – 84% = 16%. Multiply the percentage by the total to get the number of fish at the end of the year: 1,500 × 0.16 = 240. Then subtract the beginning of the year from the end of the year to calculate the increase in the number of fish: 240 – 225 = 15.

50) The correct answer is B. First, determine how many cheese and pepperoni pizzas were sold. Each triangle symbol represents 5 pizzas. Therefore, 15 cheese pizzas were sold: 3 symbols on the pictograph × 5 pizzas per symbol = 15 cheese pizzas. We also know that 10 pepperoni pizzas were sold: 2 symbols on the pictograph × 5 pizzas per symbol = 10 pepperoni pizzas. Then determine the value of these two types of pizzas based on the prices stated in the problem: (15 cheese pizzas × $10 each) + (10 pepperoni pizzas × $12 each) = $150 + $120 = $270. The remaining amount is allocable to the vegetable

pizzas: Total sales of $310 – $270 = $40 worth of vegetable pizzas. Since each triangle represents 5 pizzas, 5 vegetable pizzas were sold. We calculate the price of the vegetable pizzas as follows:

$40 worth of vegetable pizzas ÷ 5 vegetable pizzas sold = $8 per vegetable pizza

Solutions and Explanations for Practice Test Set 2 – Questions 51 to 100

51) The correct answer is B.

Factor: $x^2 - 5x + 6 \leq 0$

$(x - 2)(x - 3) \leq 0$

Then solve each parenthetical for zero:

$(x - 2) = 0$

$2 - 2 = 0$

$x = 2$

$(x - 3) = 0$

$3 - 3 = 0$

$x = 3$

So, $2 \leq x \leq 3$

Now check. Use 1 to check to $2 \leq x$, which is the same as $x \geq 2$. Since 1 is not actually greater than or equal to 2, our proof for this should be incorrect.

$x^2 - 5x + 6 \leq 0$

$1^2 - (5 \times 1) + 6 \leq 0$

$1 - 5 + 6 \leq 0$

$-4 + 6 \leq 0$

$2 \leq 0$ INCORRECT

Use 2.5 to check for $x \leq 3$. Since 2.5 really is less than 3, our proof should be correct.

$x^2 - 5x + 6 \leq 0$

$2.5^2 - (5 \times 2.5) + 6 \leq 0$

$6.25 - 12.5 + 6 \leq 0$

$-0.25 \leq 0$ CORRECT

Therefore, we have checked that $2 \leq x \leq 3$

52) The correct answer is B. Substitute 12 for the value of x. Then simplify and solve.

$x^2 + xy - y = 254$

$12^2 + 12y - y = 254$

$144 + 12y - y = 254$

$144 - 144 + 12y - y = 254 - 144$

$12y - y = 110$

$11y = 110$

$11y \div 11 = 110 \div 11$

$y = 10$

53) The correct answer is A.

FIRST: $(\boldsymbol{3x} + y)(\boldsymbol{x} - 5y) = 3x \times x = 3x^2$

OUTSIDE: $(\boldsymbol{3x} + y)(x - \boldsymbol{5y}) = 3x \times -5y = -15xy$

INSIDE: $(3x + \boldsymbol{y})(\boldsymbol{x} - 5y) = y \times x = xy$

LAST: $(3x + \boldsymbol{y})(x - \boldsymbol{5y}) = y \times -5y = -5y^2$

Then add all of the above once you have completed FOIL: $3x^2 - 15xy + xy - 5y^2 = 3x^2 - 14xy - 5y^2$

54) The correct answer is A. The factors of 9 are: $1 \times 9 = 9$; $3 \times 3 = 9$. The factors of 3 are: $1 \times 3 = 3$. So, put the integer for the common factor outside the parentheses first: $9x^3 - 3x = 3(3x^3 - x)$
Then determine if there are any common variables for the terms that remain in the parentheses. For $(3x^2 - x)$ the terms $3x^2$ and x have the variable x in common. So, now factor out x to solve: $3(3x^3 - x) = 3x(3x^2 - 1)$

55) The correct answer is C. This is a square, so to find the length of one side, we divide the perimeter by four: $36 \div 4 = 9$. Now we use the Pythagorean theorem to find the length of line segment JK. In this case JK is the hypotenuse. The hypotenuse length is the square root of $9^2 + 9^2$.
$$\sqrt{9^2 + 9^2} = \sqrt{81 + 81} = \sqrt{162}$$

56) The correct answer is A. As y increases by 5, x decreases by 5. So, if we want to determine the x coordinate for $(x, 45)$ we need to deduct 10 from the x coordinate of $(0, 35)$. Therefore, the coordinates are $(-10, 45)$, and the answer is -10.

57) The correct answer is B. Add the numbers in front of the radical signs to solve. If there is no number before the radical, then put in the number 1 because then the radical will count only 1 time when you add.
$$\sqrt{15} + 3\sqrt{15} = 1\sqrt{15} + 3\sqrt{15} = (1 + 3)\sqrt{15} = 4\sqrt{15}$$

58) The correct answer is C. In order to multiply two square roots, multiply the numbers inside the radical signs: $\sqrt{5} \times \sqrt{3} = \sqrt{5 \times 3} = \sqrt{15}$

59) The correct answer is B. Find the lowest common denominator. Then add the numerators together as shown: $\frac{x}{5} + \frac{y}{2} = \left(\frac{x}{5} \times \frac{2}{2}\right) + \left(\frac{y}{2} \times \frac{5}{5}\right) = \frac{2x}{10} + \frac{5y}{10} = \frac{2x + 5y}{10}$

60) The correct answer is D. The slope intercept formula is: $y = mx + b$. Remember that m is the slope and b is the y intercept. You will also need the slope formula: $m = \dfrac{y_2 - y_1}{x_2 - x_1}$

We are given the slope, as well as point $(4,5)$, so first we need to put those points into the slope formula. We are doing this in order to solve for b, which is not provided in the facts of the problem.
$$\frac{y_2 - y_1}{x_2 - x_1} = -\frac{3}{5}$$
$$\frac{5 - y_1}{4 - x_1} = -\frac{3}{5}$$

Then eliminate the denominator.
$$(4 - x_1)\frac{5 - y_1}{4 - x_1} = -\frac{3}{5}(4 - x_1)$$

$$5 - y_1 = -\frac{3}{5}(4 - x_1)$$

Now put in 0 for x_1 in the slope formula in order to find b, which is the y intercept (the point at which the line crosses the y axis).

$$5 - y_1 = -\frac{3}{5}(4 - x_1)$$

$$5 - y_1 = -\frac{3}{5}(4 - 0)$$

$$5 - y_1 = -\frac{3 \times 4}{5}$$

$$5 - y_1 = -\frac{12}{5}$$

$$5 - 5 - y_1 = -\frac{12}{5} - 5$$

$$-y_1 = -\frac{12}{5} - 5$$

$$-y_1 \times -1 = \left(-\frac{12}{5} - 5\right) \times -1$$

$$y_1 = \frac{12}{5} + 5$$

$$y_1 = \frac{12}{5} + \left(5 \times \frac{5}{5}\right)$$

$$y_1 = \frac{12}{5} + \frac{25}{5}$$

$$y_1 = \frac{37}{5}$$

Remember that the y intercept (known in the slope-intercept formula as the variable b) exists when x is equal to 0. We have put in the value of 0 for x in the equation above, so $b = \frac{37}{5}$. Now put the value for b into the slope intercept formula.

$$y = mx + b$$

$$y = -\frac{3}{5}x + \frac{37}{5}$$

61) The correct answer is D. Factor and cancel out if possible. Then multiply.

$$\frac{x^2 + 5x + 4}{x^2 + 6x + 5} \times \frac{16}{x + 5} =$$

$$\frac{(x + 1)(x + 4)}{(x + 1)(x + 5)} \times \frac{16}{x + 5} =$$

$$\frac{\cancel{(x + 1)}(x + 4)}{\cancel{(x + 1)}(x + 5)} \times \frac{16}{x + 5} =$$

$$\frac{(x+4)}{(x+5)} \times \frac{16}{x+5} =$$

$$\frac{(x+4) \times 16}{(x+5)(x+5)} =$$

$$\frac{16x + 64}{x^2 + 10x + 25}$$

62) The correct answer is D. When dividing fractions, you need to invert the second fraction and then multiply the two fractions together.

$$\frac{8x - 8}{x} \div \frac{3x - 3}{6x^2} = \frac{8x - 8}{x} \times \frac{6x^2}{3x - 3}$$

Then look at the numerator and denominator from the result of the previous step to see if you can factor and cancel out.

$$\frac{8x - 8}{x} \times \frac{6x^2}{3x - 3} =$$

$$\frac{8(x - 1)}{x} \times \frac{6x^2}{3(x - 1)} =$$

$$\frac{8\cancel{(x - 1)}}{x} \times \frac{6x^2}{3\cancel{(x - 1)}} =$$

$$\frac{8 \times 6x^2}{x \times 3} =$$

$$\frac{8 \times (2 \times 3 \times x \times x)}{x \times 3} =$$

$$\frac{8 \times (2 \times \cancel{3} \times \cancel{x} \times x)}{\cancel{x} \times \cancel{3}} = 16x$$

63) The correct answer is C. Any non-zero number to the power of zero is equal to 1.

64) The correct answer is B. $4^{11} \times 4^8 = 4^{(11 + 8)} = 4^{19}$

65) The correct answer is C. Perform the operation on the radicals and then simplify.
$$\sqrt{8x^4} \cdot \sqrt{32x^6} = \sqrt{8x^4 \times 32x^6} = \sqrt{256x^{10}} = \sqrt{16 \times 16 \times x^5 \times x^5} = 16x^5$$

66) The correct answer is D. Use the formula: volume = base × width × height = 20 × 15 × 25 = 7500

67) The correct answer is D. Substitute the values into the formula in order to find the solution.
$$\sqrt{A^2 + B^2} = C$$
$$\sqrt{5^2 + 12^2} = C$$
$$\sqrt{25 + 144} = C$$
$$\sqrt{169} = C$$
13 cm

68) The correct answer is C. Corresponding angles are equal in measure. So, for example, angles r and u are equal, and angles s and v are equal. Opposite angles will be equal when bisected by two parallel lines. Angles s and t are opposite, and angles u and w are also opposite. So, ∠r, ∠u, and ∠w are equal.

69) The correct answer is A. The radius of the circle is 18, so the circumference of the circle is equal to 36π. The arc length relative to the circumference is: $3\pi \div 36\pi = {}^1\!/_{12}$. We can then find the central angle as follows: $360° \div 12 = 30°$.

70) The correct answer is C. Essentially a rectangle is missing at the upper left-hand corner of the figure. We would need to know both the length and width of the "missing" rectangle in order to calculate the area of our figure. So, we need to know both X and Y in order to solve the problem.

71) The correct answer is D. The prism has 5 sides, so we need to calculate the surface area of each one. The rectangle at the bottom of the prism that lies along points, A, B, and D measures 3.5 units (side AB) by 5 units (side BD), so the surface area of the bottom rectangle is: Length × Width = $3.5 \times 5 = 17.5$ Then calculate the area of the rectangle at the back of the triangle, lying along points A and C. This rectangle measures 4 units (side AC) by 5 units (the side that is parallel to side BD). So, the area of this side is: Length × Width = $4 \times 5 = 20$. Next we need to find the length of the hypotenuse (side CB). Since AB is 3.5 units and AC is 4 units, we can use the Pythagorean theorem as follows: $\sqrt{3.5^2 + 4^2} = \sqrt{12.25 + 16} = \sqrt{28.25} \approx 5.3$. We can then calculate the surface area of the sloping rectangle that lies along the hypotenuse (along points C, B and D) as: Length × Width = $5.3 \times 5 = 26.5$ Next, we need to calculate the surface area of the two triangles on each end of the prism. The formula for the area of a triangle is $bH \div 2$, so substituting the values we get: $(3.5 \times 4) \div 2 = 7$ Finally, add the area of all five sides together to get the surface area for the entire prism: $17.5 + 20 + 26.5 + 7 + 7 = 78$

72) The correct answer is C. Volume of cylinder = $\pi R^2 h = \pi \times radius^2 \times height$. In our problem, R = 5 and h = 14. $\pi R^2 h = \pi 5^2 \times 14 = 25\pi \times 14 = 350\pi$

73) The correct answer is D. The formula for the area of a circle is: $\pi \times R^2$. First, we need to calculate the area of the larger circle: $\pi \times 2.4^2 = 5.76\pi$. Then calculate the area of the smaller inner circle: $\pi \times 1^2 = \pi$. We need to find the difference between half of each circle, so divide the area of each circle by 2 and then subtract:
$$(5.76\pi \div 2) - (\pi \div 2) = \frac{5.76\pi}{2} - \frac{\pi}{2} = \frac{4.76\pi}{2} = 2.38\pi$$

74) The correct answer is D. First, calculate the area of the central rectangle. The area of a rectangle is length times height: $8 \times 3 = 24$. Then we use the Pythagorean theorem to work out that the base of each triangle is 4.
$5 = \sqrt{3^2 + base^2}$
$5^2 = 3^2 + base^2$
$25 = 9 + base^2$
$25 - 9 = 9 - 9 + base^2$
$16 = base^2$
$4 = base$

Then calculate the area of each of the triangles on each side of the central rectangle. The area of a triangle is base times height divided by 2: $(4 \times 3) \div 2 = 6$. So, the total area is the area of the main rectangle plus the area of each of the two triangles: $24 + 6 + 6 = 36$

75) The correct answer is D. The area of a circle is π times the radius squared. Since the circles are internally tangent, the radius of circle Y is calculated by taking the radius of circle X times 2. So, the radius of circle Y is $4 \times 2 = 8$ and the area of circle Y is $8^2\pi = 64\pi$.

76) The correct answer is C. Circumference = $\pi \times 2 \times$ radius. In our question, the radius is 12, so the circumference is 24π.

77) The correct answer is B. The area of circle M is $8^2\pi = 64\pi$. The area of circle M is 39π greater than the area of circle N, so subtract to find the area of circle N: $64\pi - 39\pi = 25\pi$. The area of circle N is calculated as follows: $5^2\pi = 25\pi$. So the radius of circle N is 5.

78) The correct answer is A. Remember that the y intercept is where the line crosses the y axis, so $x = 0$ for the y intercept. Begin by substituting 0 for x.
$y = x + 14$
$y = 0 + 14$
$y = 14$
Therefore, the coordinates (0, 14) represent the y intercept.

On the other hand, the x intercept exists where the line crosses the x axis, so $y = 0$ for the x intercept. Now substitute 0 for y.
$y = x + 14$
$0 = x + 14$
$0 - 14 = x + 14 - 14$
$-14 = x$
So, the coordinates (−14, 0) represent the x intercept.

79) The correct answer is A. Our points are (5, 2) and (7, 4), so substitute the values into the midpoint formula.
$(x_1 + x_2) \div 2 , (y_1 + y_2) \div 2$
$(5 + 7) \div 2 =$ midpoint x, $(2 + 4) \div 2 =$ midpoint y
$12 \div 2 =$ midpoint x, $6 \div 2 =$ midpoint y
$6 =$ midpoint x, $3 =$ midpoint y

80) The correct answer is D. Be careful not to confuse scientific notation with logarithmic functions. In scientific notation, a number is expressed as the product of a decimal number between 1 and 10 and 10 raised to an exponential power. So, $1,200,000 = 1.2 \times 10^6$

81) The correct answer is C. y is positive even when x is negative, so we know that x is squared. We have functions with x^2 in the answer options. Looking at the value for x = 0, we can see that the output is for y is 5, so the correct function is $f(x) = x^2 + 5$.

82) The correct answer is C. Put the values provided for x into the function to solve. $f_1(2) = 5^2 = 25$

83) The correct answer is B. The principle is that $x^{-b} = \dfrac{1}{x^b}$. Therefore, $(-4)^{-3} = \dfrac{1}{-4^3} = -\dfrac{1}{64}$

84) The correct answer is C. Use the Pythagorean theorem:
$AB^2 + BC^2 = AC^2$
$AB^2 + 8^2 = 10^2$
$AB^2 + 64 = 100$
$AB^2 + 64 - 64 = 100 - 64$
$AB^2 = 36$
$AB = 6$

85) The correct answer is A. In order to calculate the mean, you simply add up the values of all of the items in the set, and then divide by the number of items in the set.
$(2 + 5 + 7 + 12 + x) \div 5 = 8$

86) The correct answer is A. To solve problems like this one, it is usually best to write out the possible outcomes in a list. This will help you visualize the number of possible outcomes that make up the sample space. Then circle or highlight the events from the list to get your answer. In this case, we have two items, each of which has a variable outcome. There are 6 numbers on the black die and 6 numbers on the red die. Using multiplication, we can see that there are 36 possible combinations: $6 \times 6 = 36$
To check your answer, you can list the possibilities of the various combinations:

(1,1)   (1,2)   (1,3)   (1,4)   (1,5)   (1,6)

(2,1)   (2,2)   (2,3)   (2,4)   (2,5)   (2,6)

(3,1)   (3,2)   (3,3)   (3,4)   (3,5)   (3,6)

(4,1)   (4,2)   (4,3)   (4,4)   (4,5)   (4,6)

(5,1)   (5,2)   (5,3)   **(5,4)**   (5,5)   (5,6)

(6,1)   (6,2)   (6,3)   (6,4)   (6,5)   (6,6)

If the number on the left in each set of parentheses represents the black die and the number on the right represents the red die, we can see that there is one chance that Sam will roll a 4 on the red die and a 5 on the black die. The result is expressed as a fraction, with the event (chance of the desired outcome) in the numerator and the total sample space (total data set) in the denominator. So, the answer is $^1/_{36}$.

87) The correct answer is D. The median is the number that is halfway through the set. Our data set is: 19, 20, 20, 15, 21, 18, 20, 23, 22, 15, 12, 23, 9, 18, 17. So first, put the numbers in ascending order: 9, 12, 15, 15, 17, 18, 18, 19, 20, 20, 20, 21, 22, 23, 23. We have 15 numbers, so the 8th number in the set is halfway and is therefore the median: 9, 12, 15, 15, 17, 18, 18, **19**, 20, 20, 20, 21, 22, 23, 23

88) The correct answer is C. The plumber is going to earn $4,000 for the month. He charges a set fee of $100 per job, and he will do 5 jobs, so we can calculate the total set fees first: $100 set fee per job × 5 jobs = $500 total set fees. Then deduct the set fees from the total for the month in order to determine the

total for the hourly pay: $4,000 − $500 = $3,500. He earns $25 per hour, so divide the hourly rate into the total hourly pay in order to determine the number of hours he will work: $3,500 total hourly pay ÷ $25 per hour = 140 hours to work

89) The correct answer is D. $\left(2 + \sqrt{6}\right)^2 = \left(2 + \sqrt{6}\right)\left(2 + \sqrt{6}\right) =$
$\left(2 \times 2\right) + \left(2 \times \sqrt{6}\right) + \left(2 \times \sqrt{6}\right) + \left(\sqrt{6} \times \sqrt{6}\right) = 4 + 4\sqrt{6} + 6 = 10 + 4\sqrt{6}$

90) The correct answer is C. Find the percentage for the patients that have not survived: 100% − 48% = 52%. Then multiply that percentage by the total for this category: 231,000 × 52% = 120,120

91) The correct answer is A. Try to find the month where all three lines look the highest. This appears to be May, November, or December. Add up the three amounts for these months to check which one is highest. May 1,400,000 + 600,000 + 400,000 = 2,400,000; November: 1,300,000 + 1,000,000 + 900,00 = 3,200,000; December: 1,500,000 + 1,000,000 + 1,000,00 = 3,500,000. So, December is the highest in total for all three companies.

92) The correct answer is A. For questions on bar graphs like this, you need to add up the bars of the same color to find the total amounts for each group. Don't worry if you are not sure of the exact amounts for each bar. Just try to get as close as possible. Here, we add up for each country as follows: Cobb County: 2.8 + 2.1 + 1.2 + 0.8 = 6.9; Dawson County: 3.5 + 1.1 + 0.9 + 2.3 = 7.8; Emery County: 2.5 + 1.8 + 1 + 0.9 = 6.2. So, 6.2 inches is the smallest amount in total.

93) The correct answer is D. You need to determine the amount of possible outcomes at the start of the day first of all. The owner has 10 brown teddy bears, 8 white teddy bears, 4 black teddy bears, and 2 pink teddy bears when she opens the attraction at the start of the day. So, at the start of the day, she has 24 teddy bears: 10 + 8 + 4 + 2 = 24. Then you need to reduce this amount by the quantity of items that have been removed. The problem tells us that she has given out a brown teddy bear, so there are 23 teddy bears left in the sample space: 24 − 1 = 23. The event is the chance of the selection of a pink teddy bear. We know that there are two pink teddy bears left after the first prize winner receives his or her prize. Finally, we need to put the event (the number representing the chance of the desired outcome) in the numerator and the number of possible remaining combinations (the sample space) in the denominator. So the answer is $^2/_{23}$.

94) The correct answer is B. Our data set is: 2.5, 9.4, 3.1, 1.7, 3.2, 8.2, 4.5, 6.4, 7.8. First, put the numbers in ascending order: 1.7, 2.5, 3.1, 3.2, 4.5, 6.4, 7.8, 8.2, 9.4. The median is the number in the middle of the set: 1.7, 2.5, 3.1, 3.2, **4.5**, 6.4, 7.8, 8.2, 9.4

95) The correct answer is D. We have the data set: 1.6, 2.9, 4.5, 2.5, 2.5, 5.1, 5.4. The mode is the number that occurs most frequently. 2.5 occurs twice, but the other numbers only occur once. So, 2.5 is the mode.

96) The correct answer is B. We don't know the age of the 10th car, so put this in as x to solve: (2 + 3 + 4 + 5 + 6 + 7 + 9 + 10 + 12 + x) ÷ 10 = 6
[(2 + 3 + 4 + 5 + 6 + 7 + 9 + 10 + 12 + x) ÷ 10] × 10 = 6 × 10
2 + 3 + 4 + 5 + 6 + 7 + 9 + 10 + 12 + x = 60
58 + x = 60

x = 2

97) The correct answer is C. First, multiply the erroneous average by the erroneous number of tests to get the total points: 78 × 8 = 624. Then divide this total by the correct amount: 624 ÷ 10 = 62.4

98) The correct answer is A. The total amount that Toby has to pay is represented by C. He is paying D dollars immediately, so we can determine the remaining amount that he owes by deducting his down payment from the total. So, the remaining amount owing is represented by the equation: C – D. We have to divide the remaining amount owing by the number of months (M) to get the monthly payment (P):
$P = (C - D) \div M = \frac{C-D}{M}$

99) The correct answer is B. Assign a variable for the age of each brother. Alex = A, Burt = B, and Zander = Z. Alex is twice as old as Burt, so A = 2B. Burt is one year older than three times the age of Zander, so B = 3Z + 1. Then substitute the value of B into the first equation.
A = 2B
A = 2(3Z + 1)
A = 6Z + 2
So, Alex is 2 years older than 6 times the age of Zander.

100) The correct answer is D. The original price of the sofa on Wednesday was *x*. On Thursday, the sofa was reduced by 10%, so the price on Thursday was 90% of *x* or 0.90*x*. On Friday, the sofa was reduced by a further 15%, so the price on Friday was 85% of the price on Thursday, so we can multiply Thursday's price by 0.85 to get our answer: (0.90)(0.85)*x*

Solutions and Explanations for Practice Test Set 3 – Questions 101 to 150

101) The correct answer is A. Expand by multiplying the terms as shown below:
FIRST: $(x - 5)(3x + 8) = x \times 3x = 3x^2$
OUTSIDE: $(x - 5)(3x + 8) = x \times 8 = 8x$
INSIDE: $(x - 5)(3x + 8) = -5 \times 3x = -15x$
LAST: $(x - 5)(3x + 8) = -5 \times 8 = -40$
Then add all of the individual results together: $3x^2 + 8x + -15x + -40 = 3x^2 - 7x - 40$

102) The correct answer is C. Isolate the integers to one side of the equation.

$$\frac{3}{4}x - 2 = 4$$

$$\frac{3}{4}x - 2 + 2 = 4 + 2$$

$$\frac{3}{4}x = 6$$

Then get rid of the fraction by multiplying both sides by the denominator.

$$\frac{3}{4}x \times 4 = 6 \times 4$$

$$3x = 24$$

Then divide to solve the problem.

$$3x \div 3 = 24 \div 3$$
$$x = 8$$

103) The correct answer is D.
Factor: $x^2 + 2x - 8 \leq 0$
$(x + 4)(x - 2) \leq 0$
Then solve each parenthetical for zero:
$(x + 4) = 0$
$-4 + 4 = 0$
$x = -4$

$(x - 2) = 0$
$2 - 2 = 0$
$x = 2$
So our solution is, $-4 \leq x \leq 2$

Now check. Use 0 to check to for $x \leq 2$. Since 0 is actually less than 2, our proof for this should be correct.
$x^2 + 2x - 8 \leq 0$
$0 + 0 - 8 \leq 0$
$-8 \leq 0$ CORRECT

Use –5 to check for –4 ≤ x. Since –4 ≤ –5 is incorrect, our proof should also be incorrect.

$x^2 + 2x - 8 \leq 0$

$-5^2 + (2 \times -5) - 8 \leq 0$

$25 - 10 - 8 \leq 0$

$25 - 18 \leq 0$

$7 \leq 0$ INCORRECT

So, we have proved that $-4 \leq x \leq 2$.

104) The correct answer is D. Notice that the equation and the inequality both contain $x - 15$. So, we can substitute y for $x - 15$ in the inequality.

$x - 15 > 0$ and $x - 15 = y$

$y > 0$

105) The correct answer is A. We know that 2 inches represents F feet. We can set this up as a ratio 2/F. Next, we need to calculate the ratio for $F + 1$. The number of inches that represents $F + 1$ is unknown, so we will refer to this unknown as x. So we have:

$$\frac{2}{F} = \frac{x}{F + 1}$$

Now cross multiply.

$$\frac{2}{F} = \frac{x}{F + 1}$$

$F \times x = 2 \times (F + 1)$

$Fx = 2(F + 1)$

Then isolate x to solve.

$Fx \div F = [2(F + 1)] \div F$

$$x = \frac{2(F + 1)}{F}$$

106) The correct answer is D. Be careful with your zeroes. We are taking 340,000 (4 zeroes) times 1,000 (three zeroes). The result is: 340,000 × 1,000 = 340,000,000 = 34 × 10,000,000 (seven zeroes). However, our answer choices are expressed with 3.4, not 34. So, we will need to multiply by a figure with 8 zeroes to account for the change in the position of the decimal.

3.4×10^8 millimeters = 3.4 × 100,000,000 millimeters = 340,000,000

107) The correct answer is A. You should use the FOIL method in this problem. Be very careful with the negative numbers when doing the multiplication.

$2(x + 2)(x - 3) =$

$2[(x \times x) + (x \times -3) + (2 \times x) + (2 \times -3)] =$

$2(x^2 + -3x + 2x + -6) =$

$2(x^2 - 3x + 2x - 6) =$

$2(x^2 - x - 6)$

Then multiply each term by the 2 at the front of the parentheses.

$2(x^2 - x - 6) =$

$2x^2 - 2x - 12$

108) The correct answer is B. Looking at this expression, we can see that each term contains x. We can also see that each term contains y. So, first factor out xy: $2xy - 6x^2y + 4x^2y^2 = xy(2 - 6x + 4xy)$. We can also see that all of the terms inside the parentheses are divisible by 2. Now let's factor out the 2. To do this, we divide each term inside the parentheses by 2: $xy(2 - 6x + 4xy) = 2xy(1 - 3x + 2xy)$

109) The correct answer is B. First, we need to calculate the shortage in the amount of houses actually built. If H represents the amount of houses that should be built and A represents the actual number of houses built, then the shortage is calculated as: $H - A$. The company has to pay P dollars per house for the shortage, so we calculate the total penalty by multiplying the shortage by the penalty per house: $(H - A) \times P$

110) The correct answer is B. Step 1: Apply the distributive property of multiplication by multiplying the first term in the first set of parentheses by all of the terms inside the second pair of parentheses. Then multiply the second term from the first set of parentheses by all of the terms inside the second set of parentheses.

$(5ab - 6a)(3ab^3 - 4b^2 - 3a) =$

$(5ab \times 3ab^3) + (5ab \times -4b^2) + (5ab \times -3a) + (-6a \times 3ab^3) + (-6a \times -4b^2) + (-6a \times -3a)$

Step 2: Add up the individual products in order to solve the problem:

$(5ab \times 3ab^3) + (5ab \times -4b^2) + (5ab \times -3a) + (-6a \times 3ab^3) + (-6a \times -4b^2) + (-6a \times -3a) =$

$15a^2b^4 - 20ab^3 - 15a^2b - 18a^2b^3 + 24ab^2 + 18a^2$

111) The correct answer is A. To divide, invert the second fraction and then multiply as shown.

$\frac{x}{5} \div \frac{9}{y} = \frac{x}{5} \times \frac{y}{9} = \frac{x \times y}{5 \times 9} = \frac{xy}{45}$

112) The correct answer is D. Place the integers on one side of the inequality.

$-3x + 14 < 5$

$-3x + 14 - 14 < 5 - 14$

$-3x < -9$

Then get rid of the negative number. We need to reverse the way that the inequality sign points because we are dividing by a negative.

$-3x < -9$

$-3x \div -3 > -9 \div -3$ ("Less than" becomes "greater than" because we divide by a negative number.)

$x > 3$

3.15 is greater than 3, so it is the correct answer.

113) The correct answer is A.

FIRST: $(\boldsymbol{x} - 2y)(\boldsymbol{2x^2} - y) = x \times 2x^2 = 2x^3$

OUTSIDE: $(\boldsymbol{x} - 2y)(2x^2 - \boldsymbol{y}) = x \times -y = -xy$

INSIDE: $(x - \boldsymbol{2y})(\boldsymbol{2x^2} - y) = -2y \times 2x^2 = -4x^2y$

LAST: $(x - \boldsymbol{2y})(2x^2 - \boldsymbol{y}) = -2y \times -y = 2y^2$

SOLUTION: $2x^3 + -xy + -4x^2y + 2y^2 = 2x^3 - 4x^2y + 2y^2 - xy$

114) The correct answer is A. Put in the values of 4 for x and -3 for y and simplify.

$2x^2 + 5xy - y^2 =$

$(2 \times 4^2) + (5 \times 4 \times -3) - (-3^2) =$

$(2 \times 4 \times 4) + (5 \times 4 \times -3) - (-3 \times -3) =$

$(2 \times 16) + (20 \times -3) - (9) =$

$32 + (-60) - 9 =$

$32 - 60 - 9 =$

$32 - 69 = -37$

115) The correct answer is C.

$6 + 8(2\sqrt{x} + 4) = 62$

$6 - 6 + 8(2\sqrt{x} + 4) = 62 - 6$

$8(2\sqrt{x} + 4) = 56$

$16\sqrt{x} + 32 = 56$

$16\sqrt{x} + 32 - 32 = 56 - 32$

$16\sqrt{x} = 24$

$16\sqrt{x} \div 16 = 24 \div 16$

$\sqrt{x} = 24 \div 16$

$\sqrt{x} = \dfrac{24}{16}$

$\sqrt{x} = \dfrac{24 \div 8}{16 \div 8} = \dfrac{3}{2}$

116) The correct answer is D. $\sqrt{18} \times \sqrt{8} = \sqrt{18 \times 8} = \sqrt{144} = \sqrt{12 \times 12} = 12$

117) The correct answer is A. Perform the multiplication on the terms in the parentheses.

$2(3x - 1) = 4(x + 1) - 3$

$6x - 2 = (4x + 4) - 3$

Then simplify.

$6x - 2 = (4x + 4) - 3$

$6x - 2 = 4x + 1$

$6x - 2 - 1 = 4x + 1 - 1$

$6x - 3 = 4x$

Then isolate x to get your answer.

$6x - 3 = 4x$

$6x - 4x - 3 = 4x - 4x$

$2x - 3 = 0$

$2x - 3 + 3 = 0 + 3$

$2x = 3$

$2x \div 2 = 3 \div 2$

$x = {}^3\!/_2$

118) The correct answer is C. The first point on the graph lies at $x = 10$, so we can eliminate answer choices A and B. The point for the y coordinate that corresponds to $x = 10$ is 63 not 68, so we can eliminate answer choice D.

119) The correct answer is B. The area of a triangle is base times height divided by 2. First, calculate the area of triangle FGJ: [6 × (8 + 10)] ÷ 2 = (6 × 18) ÷ 2 = 108 ÷ 2 = 54. Then, calculate the area of triangle FGH: (6 × 8) ÷ 2 = 24. The area of triangle FHJ is calculated by subtracting the area of triangle FGH from the area of triangle FGJ: 54 − 24 = 30

120) The correct answer is B. The measurement of a straight line is 180° so the measurement of angle A is 180° − 109° = 71°. Since this is an isosceles triangle, angle A and angle B are equal. The sum of the degrees of the three angles of any triangle is 180°, so we subtract to find the measurement of angle A: 180° − 71° − 71° = 38°.

121) The correct answer is D. Area of a circle = π × radius^2, and radius = diameter ÷ 2. Our diameter is 36, so the radius is 18. Therefore, the area is: π × radius^2 = π × 18^2 = 324π

122) The correct answer is D. Isolate the whole numbers to one side of the equation first.

$$20 - \frac{3x}{4} \geq 17$$

$$(20 - 20) - \frac{3x}{4} \geq 17 - 20$$

$$-\frac{3x}{4} \geq -3$$

Then get rid of the fraction.

$$-\frac{3x}{4} \geq -3$$

$$\left(4 \times -\frac{3x}{4}\right) \geq -3 \times 4$$

$$-3x \geq -12$$

Then deal with the remaining whole numbers.
−3x ≥ −12
−3x ÷ −3 ≥ −12 ÷ −3
x ≤ 4
Remember to reverse the way the sign points when you divide by a negative number.

123) The correct answer is D. The volume of a box is calculated by taking the length times the width times the height: 5 × 6 × 10 = 300

124) The correct answer is A. Since the diameter is 3, the circumference of this circle is 3π. The central angle in this problem is 60 degrees. So, here we are dealing with the circumference of $^1/_6$ of the circle since 60 ÷ 360 = $^1/_6$. Since the arc length is $^1/_6$ of the circumference of the circle, the arc length for this angle is: 3π ÷ 6 = $^\pi/_2$

125) The correct answer is B. The formula for perimeter is as follows: P = 2W + 2L. The patch is 12 yards by 10 yards, so we need 12 yards × 2 for the long sides patch and 10 yards × 2 for the shorter sides of the patch: (2 × 10) + (2 × 12) = 20 + 24 = 44

126) The correct answer is B. Cone volume = (π × radius^2 × height) ÷ 3
volume = (π3^2 × 4) ÷ 3 = (π9 × 4) ÷ 3 = π36 ÷ 3 = 12π

127) The correct answer is C. Use the Pythagorean theorem for the hypotenuse length $C = \sqrt{A^2 + B^2}$

$\sqrt{7^2 + B^2} = 14$

$\left(\sqrt{7^2 + B^2}\right)^2 = 14^2$

$7^2 + B^2 = 196$

$49 + B^2 = 196$

$B^2 = 196 - 49$

$B^2 = 147$

$B = \sqrt{147}$

128) The correct answer is A. We start off with point B, which is represented by the coordinates (0, 2). The line is then shifted 5 units to the left and 4 units up. When we go to the left, we need to deduct the units, and when we go up we need to add units. So, do the operations on each of the coordinates in order to solve: 0 – 5 = –5 and 2 + 4 = 6, so our new coordinates are (–5, 6).

129) The correct answer is D. The string that goes around the front, back, and sides of the package is calculated as follows: 20 + 10 + 20 + 10 = 60. The string that goes around the top, bottom, and sides of the package is calculated in the same way since the top and bottom are equal in length to the front and back: 20 + 10 + 20 + 10 = 60. So, 120 inches of string is needed so far. Then, we need 15 extra inches for the bow: 120 + 15 = 135

130) The correct answer is C. An equilateral triangle has three equal sides and three equal angles. Since all 3 angles in any triangle need to add up to 180 degrees, each angle of an equilateral triangle is 60 degrees (180 ÷ 3 = 60). Angles that lie along the same side of a straight line must add up to 180. So, we calculate angle a as follows: 180 – 60 = 120

131) The correct answers is D. The area of a circle is: πR^2. The area of circle A is $\pi \times 5^2 = 25\pi$ and the area of circle B is $\pi \times 3^2 = 9\pi$. So, the difference between the areas is 16π. The formula for circumference is: $\pi 2R$. The circumference of circle A is $\pi \times 2 \times 5 = 10\pi$ and the circumference for circle B is $\pi \times 2 \times 3 = 6\pi$. The difference in the circumferences is 4π. So, answer D is correct.

132) The correct answer is A. You need to use the distance formula: $d = \sqrt{(x_2 - x_1)^2 + (y_2 - y_1)^2}$
Put in the values provided, which were $\left(4\sqrt{7}, -2\right)$ and $(7\sqrt{7}, 4)$. Then multiply and simplify to solve.

$\sqrt{(x_2 - x_1)^2 + (y_2 - y_1)^2} =$

$\sqrt{\left(7\sqrt{7} - 4\sqrt{7}\right)^2 + (4 - -2)^2} =$

$\sqrt{\left(3\sqrt{7}\right)^2 + (6)^2} =$

$\sqrt{(9 \times 7) + 36} =$

$\sqrt{63 + 36} =$

$\sqrt{99} = \sqrt{9 \times 11} = 3\sqrt{11}$

133) The correct answer is A. y is negative when x is negative, and y is positive when x is positive. Looking at the value for x = 10, we can see that the output for y is 0.10 when x = 10, so the correct function is $f(x) = \frac{1}{x}$

134) The correct answer is D. First, solve for the function in the inner-most set of parentheses, in this case $f_1(x)$. To solve, you simply have to look at the first table. Find the value of 2 in the first column and the related value in the second column. For x = 2, $f_1(2)$ = 5. Then, take this new value to solve for $f_2(x)$. Look at the second table. Find the value of 5 in the first column and the related value in the second column. For x = 5, $f_2(5)$ = 25.

135) The correct answer is C. 0^2 = 0. All of the other answers are greater than zero.

136) The correct answer is C. Education and Public Safety are the highest. So, add these two amounts together: 27% + 21% = 48%

137) The correct answer is B. The dark gray part at the bottom of each bar represents those students who will attend the dance. 45% of the freshman, 30% of the sophomores, 38% of the juniors, and 30% of the seniors will attend. Calculating the average, we get the overall percentage for all four grades: (45 + 30 + 38 + 30) ÷ 4 = 35.75%.   35% is the closest answer to 35.75%, so it best approximates our result.

138) The correct answer is B. First of all, add up the amount of faces on the chart: 4 + 3 + 2 + 3 = 12 faces. Each face represents 10 customers, so multiply to get the total number of customers: 12 × 10 = 120 customers in total for all four regions. The salespeople received $540 in total, so we need to divide this by the amount of customers: $540 ÷ 120 customers = $4.50 per customer

139) The correct answer is A. The scores were: 9.9, 9.9, 8.2, 7.6 and 6.8. Put them in ascending order and highlight the one in the middle: 6.8, 7.6, **8.2**, 9.9, 9.9

140) The correct answer is D.
Step 1 – Determine the arithmetic mean for the data set: 150 + 149 + 124 + 103 + 99 = 625 ÷ 5 = 125
Step 2 – Calculate the "difference from the mean" for each score by subtracting the mean from each score.
Score 1: 150 – 125 = 25
Score 2: 149 – 125 = 24
Score 3: 124 – 125 = –1
Score 4: 103 – 125 = –22
Score 5: 99 – 125 = –26

Step 3 – Square the "difference from the mean" for each score.
Score 1: 25^2 = 625
Score 2: 24^2 = 576
Score 3: -1^2 = 1
Score 4: -22^2 = 484
Score 5: -26^2 = 676

Step 4 – Find the mean of the squared figures to get the variance.
625 + 576 + 1 + 484 + 676 = 2362 ÷ 5 = 472.4

Step 5 – Find the square root of the variance to get the standard deviation: $\sqrt{472.4} = 21.73$

141) The correct answer is B. The number of deserts is D and the number of main dishes is M. There are 4 family members, so both D and M are 4.

$(D \times ?) + (M \times \$8) = \$48$

$(4 \times ?) + (4 \times \$8) = \$48$

$(4 \times ?) + \$32 = \$48$

$(4 \times ?) + \$32 - \$32 = \$48 - \$32$

$4 \times ? = \$16$

$(4 \times ?) \div 4 = \$16 \div 4$

$? = \$4$

142) The correct answer is C. You need to evaluate the equation in order to determine which operations you need to perform on any new equation containing the operation ϴ and variables x and y. For the special operation $(x \ominus y) = (5x + 2y)$, in any new equation: Operation ϴ is addition; the number or variable before ϴ is multiplied by 5; the number or variable after ϴ is multiplied by 2.

So, the new equation $(6 \ominus z) = 8$ becomes $(6 \times 5) + (z \times 2) = 44$

Now solve.

$(6 \times 5) + (z \times 2) = 44$

$30 + (z \times 2) = 44$

$30 - 30 + (z \times 2) = 44 - 30$

$z \times 2 = 14$

$z = 7$

143) The correct answer is B. $y^x = Z$ is the same as $x = \log_y Z$. So, $6^3 = 216$ is the same as $3 = \log_6 216$.

144) The correct answer is A.

Step 1 – Determine the arithmetic mean for the prices: $12 + 14 + 10 + 8 = 44 \div 4 = 11$

Step 2 – Calculate the "difference from the mean" for each price.

Price 1: $12 - 11 = 1$

Price 2: $14 - 11 = 3$

Price 3: $10 - 11 = -1$

Price 4: $8 - 11 = -3$

Step 3 – Square the "difference from the mean" for each score.

Price 1: $1^2 = 1$

Price 2: $3^2 = 9$

Price 3: $-1^2 = 1$

Price 4: $-3^2 = 9$

Step 4 – Find the mean of the squared figures to get the variance.

$1 + 9 + 1 + 9 = 20 \div 4 = 5$

145) The correct answer is A. Find the total of the items in the sample space: $5 + 10 + 8 + 12 = 35$. We want to know the chance of getting an orange balloon, so put that in the denominator: $\frac{10}{35} = \frac{2}{7}$

146) The correct answer is D. We have 54 cards in the deck (13 × 4 = 52). We have taken out two spades, one heart, and a club, thereby removing 4 cards. So, the available data set is 48 (52 − 4 = 48). The desired outcome is drawing a heart. We have 13 hearts to begin with and one has been removed, so there are 12 hearts left. So, the probability of drawing a heart is $^{12}/_{48} = {}^{1}/_{4}$

147) The correct answer is C. Since there are 60 seconds in a minute, and heartbeats are measured in 10 second units, we divide the seconds as follows: 60 ÷ 10 = 6. Accordingly, the BPM is calculated by talking B times 6: BPM = B6.

148) The correct answer is D. In order to find the excess amount, we deduct the ideal BPM of 60 from the patient's actual BPM: BPM − 60

149) The correct answer is B. The two projects are being given different weights, so each project needs to have its own variable. Project X counts for 45% of the final grade, so the weighted value of project X is .45X. Project Y counts for 55%, so the weighted value of project Y is .55Y. The final grade is the total of the values for the two projects. So, we add to get our equation: .45X + .55Y

150) The correct answer is D. Set up each part of the problem as an equation. The museum had twice as many visitors on Tuesday (T) as on Monday (M), so T = 2M. The number of visitors on Wednesday exceeded that of Tuesday by 20%, so W = 1.20 × T. Then express T in terms of M for Wednesday's visitors: W = 1.20 × T = 1.20 × 2M = 2.40M. Finally, add the amounts together for all three days: M + 2M + 2.40M = 5.4M

Solutions and Explanations for Practice Test Set 4 – Questions 151 to 200

151) The correct answer is A.
Factor: $x^2 + 4x + 3 > 0$
$(x + 1)(x + 3) > 0$
Then solve each parenthetical for zero:
$(x + 1) = 0$
$-1 + 1 = 0$
$x = -1$

$(x + 3) = 0$
$-3 + 3 = 0$
$x = -3$
So, $x < -3$ or $x > -1$

Now check. Use 0 to check to for $x > -1$. Since $0 > -1$ is correct, our proof for this should also be correct.
$x^2 + 4x + 3 > 0$
$0 + 0 + 3 > 0$
$3 > 0$ CORRECT

Use -2 to check for $x < -3$. Since $-2 < -3$ is incorrect, our proof should also be incorrect.
$x^2 + 4x + 3 > 0$
$-2^2 + (4 \times -2) + 3 > 0$
$4 - 8 + 3 > 0$
$-4 + 3 > 0$
$-1 > 0$ INCORRECT

Therefore, we have checked that $x < -3$ or $x > -1$

152) The correct answer is C.
FIRST: $(\boldsymbol{x} - 9y)(\boldsymbol{x} - 9y) = x \times x = x^2$
OUTSIDE: $(\boldsymbol{x} - 9y)(x - \boldsymbol{9y}) = x \times -9y = -9xy$
INSIDE: $(x - \boldsymbol{9y})(\boldsymbol{x} - 9y) = -9y \times x = -9xy$
LAST: $(x - \boldsymbol{9y})(x - \boldsymbol{9y}) = -9y \times -9y = 81y^2$
SOLUTION: $x^2 - 18xy + 81y^2$

153) The correct answer is B. Deal with the whole numbers first.
$6 + \dfrac{x}{4} \geq 22$
$6 - 6 + \dfrac{x}{4} \geq 22 - 6$
$\dfrac{x}{4} \geq 16$

Then eliminate the fraction.
$\dfrac{x}{4} \geq 16$

$4 \times \dfrac{x}{4} \geq 16 \times 4$

$x \geq 64$

154) The correct answer is A. Perform long division of the polynomial.

```
            x + 3
x − 4)x² − x − 12
      x² − 4x
          3x − 12
          3x − 12
                0
```

155) The correct answer is A. Factor out xy: $18xy - 24x^2y - 48y^2x^2 = xy(18 - 24x - 48xy)$
Then, factor out the common factor of 6: $xy(18 - 24x - 48xy) = 6xy(3 - 4x - 8xy)$

156) The correct answer is C. Multiply the integers and add the exponents on the variables:

$\sqrt{15x^3} \times \sqrt{8x^2} =$

$\sqrt{15x^3 \times 8x^2} =$

$\sqrt{15 \times 8 \times x^3 \times x^2} =$

$\sqrt{120x^5} = \sqrt{2 \times 2 \times x^2 \times x^2 \times x \times 30} = 2x^2\sqrt{30x}$

157) The correct answer is B. We know from the second equation that y is equal to $x + 7$. So put $x + 7$ into the first equation for the value of y to solve.

$-3x - 1 = y$

$-3x - 1 = x + 7$

$-3x - 1 + 1 = x + 7 + 1$

$-3x - x = x - x + 8$

$-4x = 8$

$-4x \div -4 = 8 \div -4$

$x = -2$

Now we know that the value of x is –2, so we can put that into the equation to solve for y.

$-3x - 1 = y$

$(-3 \times -2) - 1 = y$

$6 - 1 = y$

$y = 5$

158) The correct answer is D. Any negative exponent is equal to 1 divided by the variable. So, $x^{-4} = 1 \div x^4$

159) The correct answer is C. Deal with the integers that are outside the parentheses first. Then remove the radical to solve.

$5(4\sqrt{x} - 8) = 40$

$20\sqrt{x} - 40 = 40$

$20\sqrt{x} - 40 + 40 = 40 + 40$

$20\sqrt{x} = 80$

$20\sqrt{x} \div 20 = 80 \div 20$

$\sqrt{x} = 4$

$$\sqrt{x}^2 = 4^2$$
$$x = 16$$

160) The correct answer is A. Find the cube roots of the integers and factor them. Express the result as a rational number.

$$\sqrt[3]{\frac{8}{27}} = \sqrt[3]{\frac{2 \times 2 \times 2}{3 \times 3 \times 3}} = \frac{2}{3}$$

161) The correct answer is D. When you have fractions in the numerator and denominator of another fraction, you can divide the two fractions as follows:

$$\frac{5a/b}{2a/a-b} = \frac{5a}{b} \div \frac{2a}{a-b}$$

Then invert and multiply just like you would for any other fraction.

$$\frac{5a}{b} \div \frac{2a}{a-b} = \frac{5a}{b} \times \frac{a-b}{2a} = \frac{5a^2 - 5ab}{2ab}$$

Then simplify, if possible.

$$\frac{5a^2 - 5ab}{2ab} = \frac{a(5a - 5b)}{a(2b)} = \frac{\cancel{a}(5a - 5b)}{\cancel{a}(2b)} = \frac{5a - 5b}{2b}$$

162) The correct answer is B. The line that represents the diameter of the circle forms the hypotenuse of a triangle. Side A of the triangle begins on (0, 0) and ends on (0, 2), with a length of 2. Side B of the triangle begins on (0, 2) and ends on (2, 2), so it also has a length of 2. So, the diameter of the circle is: $\sqrt{2^2 + 2^2} = \sqrt{8} = 2\sqrt{2}$. Next, we need to calculate the radius of the circle. The radius of the circle is $\sqrt{2}$ because the diameter is $2\sqrt{2}$ and the formula for the radius of a circle is ½ × diameter = radius. Finally, we can use the formula for the area of a circle to solve the problem: $\pi\sqrt{2}^2 = 2\pi$

163) The correct answer is D. A negative linear relationship exists when an increase in one variable results in a decrease in the other variable. This is represented by chart D.

164) The correct answer is D. The last 40 minutes of the journey begin at the 80 minute mark and end at the 120 minute mark. The line for 80 minutes is at 520 miles and the line for 120 minutes is at 780 miles, so the plane has traveled 260 miles (780 – 520 = 260) in the last 40 minutes. Alternatively, we can use the function that this graph represents to solve the problem. First, we can perform division to determine that the plane travels 6.5 miles per minute. For example, the line for 120 minutes is at 780 miles: 780 miles ÷ 120 minutes = 6.5 miles per minute. Since the plane is travelling at a constant rate, the graph above expresses the function: $f(x) = x \times 6.5$. So, for we can put 40 minutes in for x to solve the problem. $f(x) = x \times 6.5 = 40 \times 6.5 = 260$

165) The correct answer is B. Triangle area = (base × height) ÷ 2 = (4 × 15) ÷ 2 = 60 ÷ 2 = 30

166) The correct answer is C. Use the formula for circumference: (2 × π × radius). So, we calculate the circumference of the large circle as: 2 × π × 8 = 16π. The circumference of the small circle is: 2 × π × 5 = 10π. Then, we subtract to get our solution: 16π − 10π = 6π

167) The correct answer is A. An isosceles triangle has two equal sides, so answer A is correct. If an altitude is drawn in an isosceles triangle, we have to put a straight line down the middle of the triangle from the peak to the base. Dividing the triangle in this way would form two right triangles, rather than two equilateral triangles. So, answer B is incorrect. The base of an isosceles triangle can be longer than the length of each of the other two sides, so answer C is incorrect. The sum of all three angles of any triangle must be 180 degrees, rather than 360 degrees. So, answer D is incorrect.

168) The correct answer is A. We need to calculate the radius of the shaded portion. Since the height of the shaded portion is 6 and the height of the entire cone is 18, we know by using the rules of similarity that the ratio of the radius of the shaded portion to the radius of the entire cone is $^6/_{18}$ or $^1/_3$. Using this fraction, we can calculate the radius for the shaded portion. The radius of the entire cone is 9, so the radius of the shaded portion is 3: 9 × $^1/_3$ = 3. Then, calculate the volume of the shaded portion: $(\pi \times 3^2 \times 6) \div 3 = 54\pi \div 3 = 18\pi$

169) The correct answer is D. One side of the triangle is 18 meters and the other side of the triangle is 30 meters, so we can put these values into the formula in order to solve the problem.
$$\sqrt{A^2 + B^2} = C$$
$$\sqrt{18^2 + 30^2} = C$$
$$\sqrt{324 + 900} = C$$
$$\sqrt{1224} = C$$
35 × 35 = 1225
So, the square root of 1224 is approximately 35.

170) The correct answer is B. We can see that when x = 80, y = 60. So, when x = 160, y = 120. Alternatively, if you prefer, you can determine that the line represents the function: $f(x) = x \times 0.75$. Then substitute 160 for x: $x \times 0.75 = 160 \times 0.75 = 120$

171) The correct answer is B. Use the formula for circumference: π × radius × 2. The angle given in the problem is 30°. If we divide the total 360° in the circle by the 30° angle, we have: 360 ÷ 30 = 12. So, there are 12 such arcs along this circle. We then have to multiply the number of arcs by the length of each arc to get the circumference of the circle: 12 × 7π = 84π. Then, use the formula for the circumference of the circle to solve.
84π = π × 2 × radius
84π ÷ 2 = π × 2 × radius ÷ 2
42π = π × radius
42 = radius

172) The correct answer is A. First, calculate the total square footage available. There are 4 areas that are 10 by 10 each, so we have this equation: 4 × (10 × 10) = 400 square feet in total. Then calculate the square footage of the new offices: 20 × 10 = 200 and 2 offices × (10 × 8) = 160; 200 + 160 = 360 total

square feet for the new offices. So, the remaining square footage for the common area is determined by taking the total square footage minus the square footage of the new offices: 400 − 360 = 40 square feet remaining. Since each existing office is 10 feet long, we know that the new common area needs to be 10 feet long in order to fit in. So, the new common area is 4 feet × 10 feet.

173) The correct answer is C. Use the Pythagorean Theorem to solve. $S = \sqrt{Q^2 + R^2}$
$S = \sqrt{Q^2 + R^2} = \sqrt{3^2 + 2^2} = \sqrt{9 + 4} = \sqrt{13}$

174) The correct answer is C. Calculate the area for each of the cupboards: 8 × 2 = 16 and 5 × 2 = 10. Therefore, the total area for both cupboards is 16 + 10 = 26. Then find the area for the entire kitchen: 8 × 12 = 96. Then deduct the cupboards from the total: 96 − 26 = 70

175) The correct answer is A. First, we need to find the circumference of the semicircle on the left side of the figure. The width of the rectangle of 10 inches forms the diameter of the semicircle, so the circumference of an entire circle with a diameter of 10 inches would be 10π inches. We need the circumference for a semicircle only, which is half of a circle, so we need to divide the circumference by 2: $10\pi \div 2 = 5\pi$. Since the right side of the figure is an equilateral triangle, the two sides of the triangle have the same length as the width of the rectangle, so they are 10 inches each. Finally, you need to add up the lengths of all of the sides to get the answer: $18 + 18 + 10 + 10 + 5\pi = 56 + 5\pi$ inches

176) The correct answer is D. To solve the problem, insert the values provided into the formula for the volume of a pyramid: $\frac{1}{3}$ × length × width × height

$\frac{1}{3}$ × length × width × height = 30

$\frac{1}{3}$ × 5 × 3 × height = 30

$\frac{15}{3}$ × height = 30

5 × height = 30
5 ÷ 5 × height = 30 ÷ 5
height = 6

177) The correct answer is C.
Here is the solution for y intercept:
$5x^2 + 4y^2 = 120$
$5(0)^2 + 4y^2 = 120$
$0 + 4y^2 = 120$
$4y^2 = 120$
$4y^2 \div 4 = 120 \div 4$
$y^2 = 30$
$y = \sqrt{30}$
So, the y intercept is $(0, \sqrt{30})$

Here is the solution for x intercept:

$5x^2 + 4y^2 = 120$

$5x^2 + 4(0)^2 = 120$

$5x^2 + 0 = 120$

$5x^2 = 120$

$5x^2 \div 5 = 120 \div 5$

$x^2 = \sqrt{24}$

So the x intercept is $(\sqrt{24}, 0)$

178) The correct answer is B. Use the slope-intercept formula to calculate the slope: $y = mx + b$, where m is the slope and b is the y intercept. In our question, $x = 4$ and $y = 15$. The line crosses the y axis at 3, so put the values into the formula.

$y = mx + b$

$15 = m4 + 3$

$15 - 3 = m4 + 3 - 3$

$12 = m4$

$12 \div 4 = m$

$3 = m$

179) The correct answer is A. The perimeter of a rectangle is equal to two times the length plus two times the width. We can express this concept as an equation: $P = 2L + 2W$. Now set up formulas for the perimeters both before and after the increase.

STEP 1 – Before the increase:

$P = 2L + 2W$

$48 = 2L + 2W$

$48 \div 2 = (2L + 2W) \div 2$

$24 = L + W$

$24 - W = L + W - W$

$24 - W = L$

STEP 2 – After the increase (length is increased by 5 and width is doubled):

$P = 2L + 2W$

$92 = 2(L + 5) + (2 \times 2)W$

$92 = 2L + 10 + 4W$

$92 - 10 = 2L + 10 - 10 + 4W$

$82 = 2L + 4W$

Then solve by substitution. In this case, we substitute $24 - W$ (which we calculated in the "before" equation in step 1) for L in the "after" equation calculated in step 2, in order to solve for W.

$82 = 2L + 4W$

$82 = 2(24 - W) + 4W$

$82 = 48 - 2W + 4W$

$82 - 48 = 48 - 48 - 2W + 4W$

$82 - 48 = -2W + 4W$

$34 = -2W + 4W$

$34 = 2W$

$34 \div 2 = 2W \div 2$

$17 = W$

Then substitute the value for W in order to solve for L.

24 – W = L

24 – 17 = L

7 = L

180) The correct answer is A. $x = \log_y Z$ is the same as $y^x = Z$, so $4 = \log_4 256$ is the same as $4^4 = 256$.

181) The correct answer is B. y is positive even when x is negative, so we know we are dealing with either a squared number. Looking at the value for $x = 5$, we can see that the output for y is 32. This result can be achieved only when 2 is raised to the fifth power. So the correct function is $f(x) = 2^x$.

182) The correct answer is D. $y^x = Z$ is the same as $x = \log_y Z$, so $7^3 = 343$ is the same as $3 = \log_7 343$.

183) The correct answer is D. Put the values provided for x into the function to solve.

$f_1 = x^2 + x = 5^2 + 5 = 25 + 5 = 30$

184) The correct answer is D. Look at the bars for June 1 at the far right side of the graph. First, find the total amount of accidents on that date. Cars were involved in 30 accidents, vans in 20 accidents, pick-ups in 10 accidents, and SUV's in 5 accidents. So, there were 65 accidents in total (30 + 20 + 10 + 5 = 65). Then divide the number of accidents for pick-ups and vans into the total: $30 \div 65 = 46.1538\% \approx 46\%$

185) The correct answer is C. There are 2 stars for speeding, and each star equals 30 violations, so there were 60 speeding violations in total. The fine for speeding is $50 per violation, so the total amount collected for speeding violations was: 60 speeding violations × $50 per violation = $3000. There are three stars for other violations, which is equal to 90 violations (3 × 30 = 90). Other violations are $20 each, so the total for other violations is: 90 × $20 = $1800. Next, we need to deduct these two amounts from the total collections of $6,000 to find the amount collected for parking violations: $6000 – $3000 – $1800 = $1200 in total for parking violations. There is one star for parking violations, so there were 30 parking violations. We divide to get the answer: $1200 income for parking violations ÷ 30 parking violations = $40 each

186) The correct answer is D. The most striking relationship on the graph is the line for ages 65 and over, which clearly shows a negative relationship between exercising outdoors and the number of days of rain per month. You will recall that a negative relationship exists when an increase in one variable causes a decrease in the other variable. So, we can conclude that people aged 65 and over seem less inclined to exercise outdoors when there is more rain.

187) The correct answer is C. We need to use the formula to calculate the length of the arc: s = r θ Remember that θ = the radians of the subtended angle, s = arc length, and r = radius. So, substitute values into the formula to solve the problem. In our problem: radius (r) = 16 and radians (θ) = $^{3\pi}/_4$

s = r θ; s = 16 × $^{3\pi}/_4$ = 12π

188) The correct answer is A. The range is the highest amount minus the lowest amount: 21 – 3 = 18

189) The correct answer is B. Two members have lost 12 kilograms, and all of the other amounts occur only one time each. So, 12 is the mode.

190) The correct answer is C. Let's say the number widgets is represented by D and the number whatsits is represented by H. Your equation is: (D × $2) + (H × $25) = $85. We know that the number of whatsits is 3, so put that in the equation and solve for the number of widgets.

(D × $2) + (H × $25) = $85

(D × $2) + (3 × $25) = $85

(D × $2) + $75 = $85

(D × $2) + 75 − 75 = $85 − $75

(D × $2) = $10

$2D = $10

$2D ÷ 2 = $10 ÷ 2

D = 5

191) The correct answer is A. To find the median, first of all you need to put the numbers is ascending order: 2, 2, 3, 5, **6**, **8**, 8, 10, 12, 21. Here, we have got an even number of items, so we need to take an average of the two items in the middle: (8 + 6) ÷ 2 = 7

192) The correct answer is C. If all of the values in a data set are positive integers greater than zero and all of the values increase, the mean and median will also increase, but the range will not change. Conversely, if all of the values in such a data set decrease, the mean and median will also decrease, but the range will not change. If each number in the set is increased by 2, the mean will increase by 2 since the overall increase in the total of the values (2 × 9 = 18) will be divided equally among all nine items in the set (18 ÷ 9 = 2) when the mean is calculated. Since each of the numbers increases by 2, the median number will also increase by 2.

193) The correct answer is B. This question is asking you to determine the value missing from a sample space when calculating basic probability. This is like other problems on basic probability, but we need to work backwards to find the missing value. First, set up an equation to find the total items in the sample space. Then subtract the quantities of the known subsets from the total in order to determine the missing value. We will use variable T as the total number of items in the set. The probability of getting a red ribbon is $1/3$. So, set up an equation to find the total items in the data set:

$$\frac{5}{T} = \frac{1}{3}$$

$$\frac{5}{T} \times 3 = \frac{1}{3} \times 3$$

$$\frac{5}{T} \times 3 = 1$$

$$\frac{15}{T} = 1$$

$$\frac{15}{T} \times T = 1 \times T$$

$$15 = T$$

We have 5 red ribbons, 6 blue ribbons, and x green ribbons in the data set that make up the total sample space, so now subtract the amount of red and blue ribbons from the total in order to determine the number of green ribbons.

$5 + 6 + x = 15$

$11 + x = 15$

$11 - 11 + x = 15 - 11$

$x = 4$

194) The correct answer is A. Miles per hour (MPH) is calculated as follows: miles ÷ hours = MPH. So, if we have the MPH and the miles traveled, we need to change the above equation in order to calculate the hours.

miles ÷ hours = MPH

miles ÷ hours × hours = MPH × hours

miles = MPH × hours

miles ÷ MPH = (MPH × hours) ÷ MPH

miles ÷ MPH = hours

In other words, we divide the number of miles by the miles per hour to get the time for each part of the event. So, for the first part of the event, the hours are calculated as follows: 80 ÷ 5. For the second part of the event, we take the remaining mileage and divide by the unknown variable: 20 ÷ x. Since the event is divided into two parts, these two results added together equal the total time.

Total time = [(80 ÷ 5) + (20 ÷ x)]

The total amount of miles for the event is then divided by the total time to get the average miles per hour for the entire event. We have a 100 mile endurance event, so the result is: 100 ÷ [(80 ÷ 5) + (20 ÷ x)]

195) The correct answer is D. Probability can be expressed as a decimal or a proper fraction. Probability cannot be a negative number or a number greater than 1. So, the correct answer is D.

196) The correct answer is C. We know that she traveled 150 miles before the repair. Miles traveled before needing the repair: 60 MPH × 2.5 hours = 150 miles traveled. If the journey is 240 miles in total, she has 90 miles remaining after the car is repaired: 240 − 150 = 90. If she then travels at 75 miles an hour for 90 miles, the time she spends is: 90 ÷ 75 = 1.2 hours. There are 60 minutes in an hour, so 1.2 hours is 1 hour and 12 minutes because 60 minutes × 0.20 = 12 minutes. The time spent traveling after the repair is 1 hour and 12 minutes. Now add together all of the times to get your answer: Time spent before needing the repair: 2.5 hours = 2 hours and 30 minutes; Time spent waiting for the repair: 2 hours; The time spent traveling after the repair: 1 hour and 12 minutes; Total time: 5 hours and 42 minutes. If she left home at 6:00 am, she will arrive at her mother's house at 11:42 am.

197) The correct answer is C. If the amount earned from selling jackets was one-third that of selling jeans, the ratio of jacket to jean sales was 1 to 3. So, we need to divide the total sales of $4,000 into $1,000 for jackets and $3,000 for jeans. We can then solve as follows:

$3,000 in jeans sales ÷ $20 per pair = 150 pairs sold

198) The correct answer is D. Divide each side of the equation by 3. Then subtract 5 from both sides of the equation as shown below.

18 = 3(x + 5)

18 ÷ 3 = [3(x + 5)] ÷ 3

6 = x + 5
6 − 5 = x + 5 − 5
1 = x

199) The correct answer is D. First, we have to calculate the output for our first production method for 10 days: D^5 + 12,000 = 10^5 + 12,000 = 100,000 + 12,000 = 112,000
Then we have to calculate the output for the other production method: 10 × 10,000 = 100,000
112,000 is greater than the 100,000 amount for method B yields.
So, the greatest amount of production for 10 days is 112,000 bottles.

200) The correct answer is D. The first three bars of the graph represent the first 30 minutes, so add these three amounts together for your answer: 1.5 + 1.2 + 0.8 = 3.5 miles

Solutions and Explanations for Practice Test Set 5 – Questions 201 to 250

201) The correct answer is C.
$(5x - 2)(3x^2 + 5x - 8) =$
$(5x \times 3x^2) + (5x \times 5x) + (5x \times -8) + (-2 \times 3x^2) + (-2 \times 5x) + (-2 \times -8) =$
$15x^3 + 25x^2 - 40x - 6x^2 - 10x + 16 =$
$15x^3 + 25x^2 - 6x^2 - 40x - 10x + 16 =$
$15x^3 + 19x^2 - 50x + 16$

202) The correct answer is A. You can subtract the second equation from the first equation as the first step in solving the problem. Look at the term containing x in the second equation. $8x$ is in the second equation. In order to eliminate the term containing x, we need to multiply the first equation by 8.
$x + 5y = 24$
$(x \times 8) + (5y \times 8) = 24 \times 8$
$8x + 40y = 192$

Now subtract.
$$8x + 40y = 192$$
$$\underline{- (8x + 2y = 40)}$$
$$38y = 152$$

Then solve for y.
$38y = 152$
$38y \div 38 = 152 \div 38$
$y = 4$

Now put the value for y into the first equation and solve for x.
$x + 5y = 24$
$x + (5 \times 4) = 24$
$x + 20 = 24$
$x = 4$
$x = 4$ and $y = 4$, so the answer is (4, 4).

203) The correct answer is C. Find the lowest common denominator. Then add the numerators and simplify.
$$\frac{2}{10x} + \frac{3}{12x^2} =$$
$$\left(\frac{2 \times 6x}{10x \times 6x}\right) + \left(\frac{3 \times 5}{12x^2 \times 5}\right) =$$
$$\frac{12x}{60x^2} + \frac{15}{60x^2} = \frac{12x + 15}{60x^2} =$$
$$\frac{3(4x + 5)}{3 \times 20x^2} = \frac{\cancel{3}(4x + 5)}{\cancel{3} \times 20x^2} = \frac{4x + 5}{20x^2}$$

204) The correct answer is B. Factor the integers inside each of the square root signs. Then find a perfect square for one of the factors for each radical.
$\sqrt{50} + 4\sqrt{32} + 7\sqrt{2} =$

$\sqrt{25 \times 2} + 4\sqrt{16 \times 2} + 7\sqrt{2} =$

$5\sqrt{2} + (4 \times 4)\sqrt{2} + 7\sqrt{2} =$

$5\sqrt{2} + 16\sqrt{2} + 7\sqrt{2} = 28\sqrt{2}$

205) The correct answer is C. First perform the division on the integers: $10 \div 2 = 5$
Then do the division on the other variables.

$a^2 \div a = a$

$b^3 \div b^2 = b$

$c \div c^2 = \dfrac{1}{c}$

Then multiply these results to get the solution.

$5 \times a \times b \times \dfrac{1}{c} = \dfrac{5ab}{c} = 5ab \div c$

206) The correct answer is B. Find the lowest common denominator.

$\dfrac{\sqrt{48}}{3} + \dfrac{5\sqrt{5}}{6} = \left(\dfrac{\sqrt{48}}{3} \times \dfrac{2}{2}\right) + \dfrac{5\sqrt{5}}{6} = \dfrac{2\sqrt{48}}{6} + \dfrac{5\sqrt{5}}{6}$

Then simplify, if possible.

$\dfrac{2\sqrt{48}}{6} + \dfrac{5\sqrt{5}}{6} = \dfrac{2\sqrt{(4 \times 4) \times 3}}{6} + \dfrac{5\sqrt{5}}{6} = \dfrac{(2 \times 4)\sqrt{3} + 5\sqrt{5}}{6} = \dfrac{8\sqrt{3} + 5\sqrt{5}}{6}$

207) The correct answer is B. Substitute 1 for x: $\dfrac{x-3}{2-x} = \dfrac{1-3}{2-1} = (1 - 3) \div (2 - 1) = -2 \div 1 = -2$

208) The correct answer is D. Multiply the amounts inside the radical sign, but leave the cube root as it is:

$\sqrt[3]{5} \times \sqrt[3]{7} = \sqrt[3]{35}$

209) The correct answer is D. Simplify the numerator and multiply the radicals in the denominator using the FOIL method. Then simplify the denominator.

$\dfrac{1}{\sqrt{x} - \sqrt{y}} \times \dfrac{\sqrt{x} + \sqrt{y}}{\sqrt{x} + \sqrt{y}} = \dfrac{\sqrt{x} + \sqrt{y}}{\sqrt{x}^2 + \sqrt{xy} - \sqrt{xy} - \sqrt{y}^2} = \dfrac{\sqrt{x} + \sqrt{y}}{\sqrt{x}^2 - \sqrt{y}^2} = \dfrac{\sqrt{x} + \sqrt{y}}{x - y}$

210) The correct answer is D. Factor each of the parentheticals in the expression: $(3x + 3y)(5a + 5b) = 3(x + y) \times 5(a + b)$. We know that $x + y = 5$ and $a + b = 4$, so we can substitute the values for each of the parentheticals: $3(x + y) \times 5(a + b) = 3(5) \times 5(4) = 15 \times 20 = 300$

211) The correct answer is D.
Step 1: Factor the equation.
$x^2 + 6x + 8 = 0$
$(x + 2)(x + 4) = 0$
Step 2: Now substitute 0 for x in the first pair of parentheses.
$(0 + 2)(x + 4) = 0$
$2(x + 4) = 0$
$2x + 8 = 0$

$2x + 8 - 8 = 0 - 8$

$2x = -8$

$2x \div 2 = -8 \div 2$

$x = -4$

Step 3: Then substitute 0 for x in the second pair of parentheses.

$(x + 2)(x + 4) = 0$

$(x + 2)(0 + 4) = 0$

$(x + 2)4 = 0$

$4x + 8 = 0$

$4x + 8 - 8 = 0 - 8$

$4x = -8$

$4x \div 4 = -8 \div 4$

$x = -2$

212) The correct answer is C. The line in a fraction is the same as the division symbol. For example, $^a/_b = a \div b$. In the same way, $^3/_{xy} = 3 \div (xy)$.

213) The correct answer is D. Get the integers to one side of the equation first of all.

$\dfrac{1}{5}x + 3 = 5$

$\dfrac{1}{5}x + 3 - 3 = 5 - 3$

$\dfrac{1}{5}x = 2$

Then multiply to eliminate the fraction and solve the problem.

$\dfrac{1}{5}x \times 5 = 2 \times 5$

$x = 10$

214) The correct answer is C.

Factor: $x^2 - 12x + 35 < 0$

$(x - 7)(x - 5) < 0$

Then solve each parenthetical for zero:

$(x - 7) = 0$

$7 - 7 = 0$

$x = 7$

$(x - 5) = 0$

$5 - 5 = 0$

$x = 5$

So, $5 < x < 7$

Now check. Use 6 to check to for $x < 7$. Since $6 < 7$ is correct, our proof for this should also be correct.

$x^2 - 12x + 35 < 0$

$6^2 - (12 \times 6) + 35 < 0$

$36 - 72 + 35 < 0$

$-36 + 35 < 0$

$-1 < 0$ CORRECT

Use 4 to check for x > 5, which is the same as 5 < x. Since 4 > 5 is incorrect, our proof for this should be incorrect.

$x^2 - 12x + 35 < 0$

$4^2 - (12 \times 4) + 35 < 0$

$16 - 48 + 35 < 0$

$-32 + 35 < 0$

$3 < 0$ INCORRECT

So, we have proved that 5 < x < 7.

215) The correct answer is C. Each term contains the variables x and y. So, factor out *xy* as shown: $2xy - 8x^2y + 6y^2x^2 = xy(2 - 8x + 6xy)$. Then, factor out any whole numbers. All of the terms inside the parentheses are divisible by 2, so factor out 2: $xy(2 - 8x + 6xy) = 2xy(1 - 4x + 3xy)$

216) The correct answer is D. When looking at scatterplots, try to see if the dots are roughly grouped into any kind of pattern or line. If so, positive or negative relationships may be represented. Here, however, the dots are located at what appear to be random places on all four quadrants of the graph. So, the scatterplot suggests that there is no relationship between x and y.

217) The correct answer is C. The formula for circumference is: $\pi \times 2 \times R$. The center of the circle is on (0, 0) and the top edge of the circle extends to (0, 3), so the radius of the circle is 3. Therefore, the circumference is: $\pi \times 2 \times 3 = 6\pi$

218) The correct answer is B. The base of the garage is square, so its volume is calculated by taking the length times the width times the height: $20 \times 20 \times 18 = 7200$. The roof of the garage is a pyramid shape, so its volume is calculated by taking one-third of the base length squared times the height: $(20 \times 20 \times 15) \times \frac{1}{3} = 6000 \div 3 = 2000$. So, the volume of the roof to the volume of the base is: $\frac{2000}{7200} = \frac{5}{18}$

219) The correct answer is B. Circumference is $2\pi R$, so the circumference of the large wheel is 20π and the circumference of the smaller wheel is 12π. If the large wheel travels 360 revolutions, it travels a distance of: $20\pi \times 360 = 7200\pi$. To determine the number of revolutions the small wheel needs to make to go the same distance, we divide the distance by the circumference of the smaller wheel: $7200\pi \div 12\pi = 600$. Finally, calculate the difference in the number of revolutions: $600 - 360 = 240$

220) The correct answer is A. The diameter of the circle is 2, so the circumference is 2π. There are 360 degrees in a circle and the question is asking us about a 20 degree angle, so the arc length relates to one-eighteenth of the circumference: $20 \div 360 = \frac{1}{18}$. So, we need to take one-eighteenth of the circumference to get the answer: $2\pi \times \frac{1}{18} = \frac{2\pi}{18} = \frac{\pi}{9}$

221) The correct answer is B. The two sides of the field form a right angle, so we can use the Pythagorean theorem to solve the problem: $\sqrt{3^2 + 4^2} = \sqrt{9 + 16} = \sqrt{25} = 5$

222) The correct answer is A. Since the left and right sides of this figure are not parallel, the figure is classified as a trapezoid. To find the area of a trapezoid we take the average of the length of the top (T) and bottom (B) and multiply by the height (H):
$\frac{T+B}{2} \times H = \frac{7+12}{2} \times 6 = 9.5 \times 6 = 57$

223) The correct answer is D. To find the area of the rectangle, we must first find the missing length of the one side by subtracting: 15 − 6 = 9. Then multiply to find the area of the rectangle: 9 × 5 = 45. Then find the area of the triangle: (6 × 5) ÷ 2 = 15. Finally, add to find the total area: 45 + 15 = 60.

224) The correct answer is C. The answer is the radian equation for 90 degrees: $\pi \div 2 \times$ radian = 90°

225) The correct answer is C. We simply divide to get the answer: 64 ÷ 4 = 16

226) The correct answers is B. A parallelogram is a four-sided figure that has two pairs of parallel sides. The opposite or facing sides of a parallelogram are of equal length and the opposite angles of a parallelogram are of equal measure. You will recall that congruent is another word for equal in measure. So, answer B is correct. A rectangle is a parallelogram with four angles of equal size (all of which are right angles), while a square is a parallelogram with four sides of equal length and four right angles.

227) The correct answer is B. Two angles are supplementary if they add up to 180 degrees.

228) The correct answer is A. The problem tells us that A is 3 times B, and B is 3 more than 6 times C. So, we need to create equations based on this information.
B is 3 more than 6 times C: B = 6C + 3
A is 3 times B: A = 3B
Since B = 6C + 3, we can substitute 6C + 3 for B in the second equation as follows:
A = 3B
A = 3(6C + 3)
A = 18C + 9
So, A is 9 more than 18 times C.

229) The correct answer is C. Looking at the value for x = 100, we can see that the output for y is 10. We can get this result only when the output is the square root of x. so the correct function is $f(x) = \sqrt{x}$

230) The correct answer is C. $x = \log_y Z$ is the same as $y^x = Z$, so $2 = \log_8 64$ is the same as $8^2 = 64$.

231) The correct answer is B. $y^x = Z$ is the same as $x = \log_y Z$, so $9^2 = 81$ is the same as $2 = \log_9 81$.

232) The correct answer is B. Put the values provided for x into the second function. $f_2(9) = \sqrt{9} + 3 = 3 + 3 = 6$. Then put this result into the first function. $f_1(6) = 3 \times 6 + 1 = 19$

233) The correct answer is C. The question is asking us how many residents have more than 3 relatives nearby, so we need to add the bars for 4 and 5 relatives from the chart. 20 residents have 4 relatives nearby and 10 residents have 5 relatives nearby, so 30 residents (20 + 10 = 30) have more than 3 relatives nearby.

234) The correct answer is A. Find the amount of items in the sample set before anything is removed from the set: 4 + 2 + 1 + 4 + 5 = 16. One piece of rope has been removed, so deduct that from the sample space for the second draw: 16 − 1 = 15. The box originally had 4 pieces of blue rope, and one piece of blue rope has been removed, so there are 3 pieces of blue rope available for the second draw. So, the probability is $^3/_{15} = ^1/_5$

235) The correct answer is D. Questions like this one are asking you about how to express percentages graphically. Facts such as x students from y total students participate in a group can be represented as $^x/_y$. Ten out of 25 students participate in drama club. First of all, express the relationship as a fraction: $^{10}/_{25}$. Then divide to find the percentage: $^{10}/_{25} = 10 \div 25 = 0.40 = $ 40%. Finally, choose the pie chart that has 40% of its area shaded in dark gray. 40% is slightly less than half, so you need to choose chart D.

236) The correct answer is C. This is an example of a question that asks you to interpret a graph in order to determine the price per unit of an item. To solve the problem, look at the graph and then divide the total sales in dollars by the total quantity sold in order to get the price per unit. For ten hamburgers, the total price is $85, so each hamburger sells for $8.50: $85 total sales in dollars ÷ 10 hamburgers sold = $8.50 each

237) The correct answer is D. Our points are (5, 7) and (11, −3) and the midpoint formula is:
$(x_1 + x_2) \div 2 , (y_1 + y_2) \div 2$
(5 + 11) ÷ 2 = midpoint x, (7 − 3) ÷ 2 = midpoint y
16 ÷ 2 = midpoint x, 4 ÷ 2 = midpoint y
8 = midpoint x, 2 = midpoint y

238) The correct answer is C. In order to find the value of a variable inside a square root sign, you need to square each side of the equation.
$\sqrt{9z + 18} = 9$
$\sqrt{9z + 18}^2 = 9^2$
$9z + 18 = 81$
$9z + 18 - 18 = 81 - 18$
$9z = 63$
$9z \div 9 = 63 \div 9$
$z = 7$

239) The correct answer is C. First you need to get rid of the fraction. To eliminate the fraction, multiply each side of the equation by the denominator of the fraction.
$z = \dfrac{x}{1 - y}$
$z \times (1 - y) = \dfrac{x}{1 - y} \times (1 - y)$

$z(1 - y) = x$

Then isolate y to solve.

$z(1 - y) \div z = x \div z$

$1 - y = x \div z$

$1 - 1 - y = (x \div z) - 1$

$-y = (x \div z) - 1$

$-y \times -1 = [(x \div z) - 1] \times -1$

$y = -\dfrac{x}{z} + 1$

240) The correct answer is D. Multiply the radical in front of the parentheses by each radical inside the parentheses. Then simplify further if possible.

$\sqrt{6} \cdot (\sqrt{40} + \sqrt{6}) =$

$(\sqrt{6} \times \sqrt{40}) + (\sqrt{6} \times \sqrt{6}) =$

$\sqrt{240} + 6 = \sqrt{16 \times 15} + 6 = 4\sqrt{15} + 6$

241) The correct answer is C. When you have fractions as exponents, the denominator of the faction is placed in front of the radical sign. The numerators become the new exponents:

$a^{1/2} b^{1/4} c^{3/4} = \sqrt{a} \times \sqrt[4]{b} \times \sqrt[4]{c}^3$

242) The correct answer is A. If the base is the same, and you need to divide, you subtract the exponents: $ab^8 \div ab^2 = ab^{8-2} = ab^6$

243) The correct answer is C. For questions that ask you to interpret bar graphs, you need to read the problem carefully to determine what is represented on the horizontal axis (bottom) and the vertical axis (left side) of the graph. The quantity of diseases is indicated on the bottom of the graph, while the number of children is indicated on the left side of the graph. To determine the amount of children that have been vaccinated against three or more diseases, we need to add the amounts represented by the bars for 3, 4, and 5 diseases: 30 + 20 + 10 = 60 children

244) The correct answer is B. The range is the highest amount minus the lowest amount: 91 − 54 = 37

245) The correct answer is A. What do we do when no number appears in the set more than once? If no number is duplicated, then we say that the data set has no mode.

246) The correct answer is A. Find the total points for the first group: 50 × 82 = 4100. Then find the total points for the second group. 50 × 89 = 4450. Add these two amounts together for the total points: 4100 + 4450 = 8550. Then divide the total points by the total amount of members in the group: 8550 ÷ 10 = 85.5

247) The correct answer is C. Put the scores in ascending order: 32, 38, **40**, **45**, 46, 49. Because there is an even number of items in the set, we take the average of the two middle values: (40 + 45) ÷ 2 = 42.5

248) The correct answer is D. Find the lowest common denominator.

$$\dfrac{1}{a + 1} + \dfrac{1}{a} =$$

$$\left(\frac{1}{a+1} \times \frac{a}{a}\right) + \left(\frac{1}{a} \times \frac{a+1}{a+1}\right) =$$

$$\frac{a}{a^2+a} + \frac{a+1}{a^2+a}$$

Then simplify, if possible

$$\frac{a}{a^2+a} + \frac{a+1}{a^2+a} =$$

$$\frac{a+a+1}{a^2+a} = \frac{2a+1}{a^2+a}$$

249) The correct answer is D. Treat the main fraction as the division sign.

$$\frac{5x}{1/xy} = 5x \div \frac{1}{xy}$$

Then invert the second fraction and multiply as usual.

$$5x \div \frac{1}{xy} = 5x \times \frac{xy}{1} = 5x \times xy = 5x^2y$$

250) The correct answer is B. Convert the seconds to hours: 108,000 seconds ÷ 60 seconds per minute ÷ 60 minutes per hour = 30 hours. Then multiply by the speed of the rocket to get the miles: 25,000 miles per hour × 30 hours = 750,000 miles to travel. Finally, express your answer in scientific notation: $750{,}000 = 7.5 \times 100{,}000 = 7.5 \times 10^5$

Extra Practice Questions:

Look at the diagram below and answer questions 251 to 254

Brooke wants to put new flooring in her living room. She will buy the flooring in square pieces that measure 1 square foot each. The entire room is 8 feet by 12 feet. The bookcases are two feet deep from front to back. Flooring will not be put under the bookcases. Each piece of flooring costs $5.50. A diagram of her living room is provided.

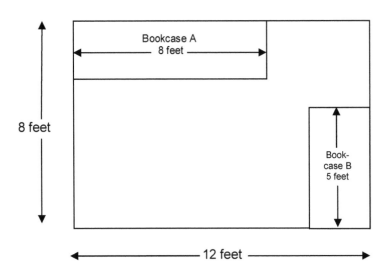

251)   What is the area of the floor surface below bookcase A?
   A) 8 square feet
   B) 16 square feet
   C) 20 square feet
   D) 64 square feet

252)   What is the area of the floor surface below bookcase B?
   A) 5 square feet
   B) 10 square feet
   C) 14 square feet
   D) 25 square feet

253)   How much will Brooke pay to cover her living room floor?
   A) $350
   B) $385
   C) $480
   D) $528

254)   If Brooke gets a 27.5% discount off the $5.50 price per tile, how much will she pay to cover her living room floor?
   A) $105.88
   B) $253.75
   C) $279.13
   D) $382.80

Look at the table below and answer questions 255 to 257.

Disease or Complication	Percentage of patients with this disease that have survived and total number of patients
Cardiopulmonary and vascular	82% (602,000)
HIV/AIDS	73% (215,000)
Diabetes	89% (793,000)
Cancer and leukemia	48% (231,000)
Premature birth complications	64% (68,000)

255)   Approximately how many patients with diabetes have survived?
    A) 58,050   B) 87,230   C) 156,950   D) 705,770

256)   The highest number of deaths occurred as a result of which disease?
    A) Cardiovascular an pulmonary disease
    B) HIV/AIDS
    C) Cancer and leukemia
    D) Premature birth complications

257)   The total number of deaths from the two least fatal diseases amounted to which figure below?
    A) 82,530   B) 208,960   C) 1,186,040   D) 1,199,410

Look at the graph below and answer questions 258 to 261.

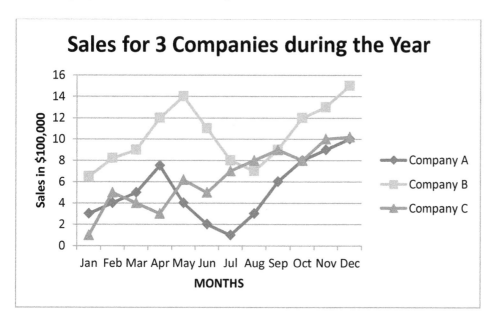

258)   Which company had the highest sales figure for July?
    A) Company A   B) Company B   C) Company C   D) Companies B and C

259) What was the approximate sales figure for Company A for April?
    A) $300,000   B) $500,000   C) $790,000   D) $1,200,000

260) What was the approximate difference in sales for Company B and Company C in May?
    A) Company B's sales were $800,000 more than Company C's.
    B) Company C's sales were $800,000 more than Company B's.
    C) Company B's sales were $80,000 less than Company C's.
    D) Company C's sales were $80,000 less than Company B's.

261) The combined total of sales for all three of the companies was greatest during which month of the year?
    A) December   B) November   C) May   D) April

Look at the bar chart below and answer questions 262 to 264.

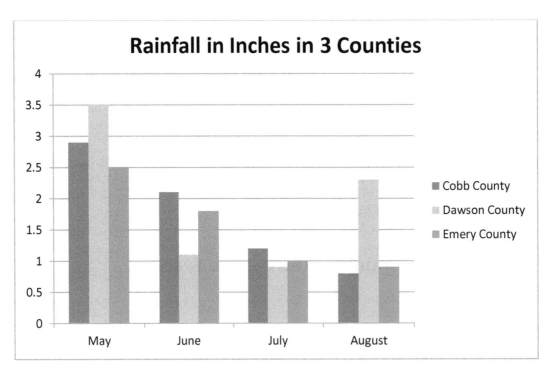

262) Approximately how many inches of rainfall did Cobb County have for July and August in total?
    A) 0.7 inches   B) 0.9 inches   C) 2 inches   D) 3.2 inches

263) What was the approximate difference in the amount of rainfall for Dawson County and Emery County for June?
    A) Dawson County had 0.6 more inches of rainfall than Emery County.
    B) Emery County had 0.6 more inches of rainfall than Dawson County.
    C) Dawson County had 1.1 fewer inches of rainfall than Emery County.
    D) Emery County had 1.1 fewer inches of rainfall than Dawson County.

264) What was the approximate total rainfall for Emery County for all four months?
    A) 6.2 inches   B) 6.8 inches   C) 7.0 inches   D) 7.4 inches

Look at the pie chart and information below and answer questions 265 to 267.

A zoo has reptiles, birds, quadrupeds, and fish. At the start of the year, they have a total of 1,500 creatures living in the zoo. The pie chart below shows percentages by category for the 1,500 creatures at the start of the year. At the end of the year, the zoo still has 1,500 creatures, but reptiles constitute 40%, quadrupeds 21%, and fish 16%.

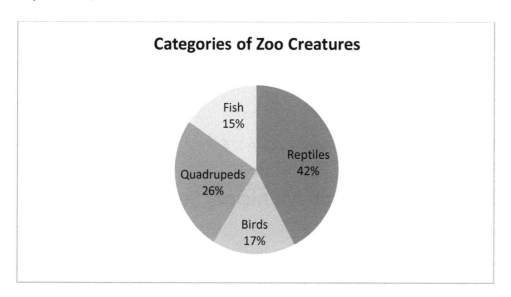

Categories of Zoo Creatures

265) How many reptiles are in the zoo at the start of the year?
A) 225
B) 255
C) 390
D) 630

266) What was the difference between the number of quadrupeds at the start of the year and the number of fish at the start of the year?
A) There were 165 more fish than quadrupeds.
B) There were 165 more quadrupeds than fish.
C) There were 75 more fish than quadrupeds.
D) There were 75 more quadrupeds than fish.

267) What can be said about the number of birds at the end of the year when compared to the number of birds at the beginning of the year?
A) There were 23 more birds at the end of the year than at the beginning of the year.
B) There were 23 fewer birds at the end of the year than at the beginning of the year.
C) There were 90 more birds at the end of the year than at the beginning of the year.
D) There were 90 fewer birds at the end of the year than at the beginning of the year.

Look at the table below and answer questions 268 to 272.

Sunday	Monday	Tuesday	Wednesday	Thursday	Friday	Saturday
−10°F	−9°F	1°F	6°F	8°F	13°F	12°F

268) What was the difference between the temperature on Sunday and the temperature on Saturday?
A) 22°   B) 23°   C) 2°   D) −2°

269) What was the median temperature for the week?
A) 1°   B) 3°   C) 6°   D) 22°

270) What was the mean temperature for the week?
A) 1°   B) 3°   C) 6°   D) 22°

271) What was the mode in the temperatures for the week?
A) 1°   B) 3°   C) 8°   D) no mode

272) What is the range in the temperatures for the week?
A) −2°   B) −3°   C) −23°   D) 23°

Look at the pie chart below and answer questions 273 to 275.

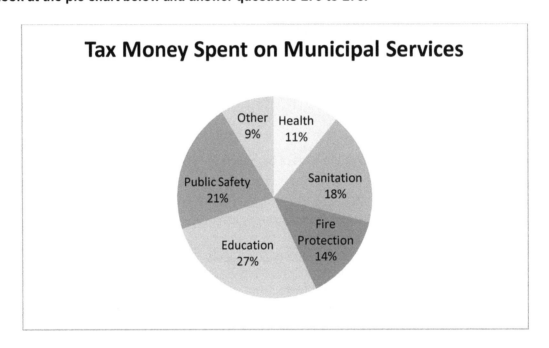

273) According to the chart, the two lowest categories accounted for what percentage of use in total?
A) 18%   B) 20%   C) 23%   D) 29%

274) If $5,275,300 in total tax money was spend on all municipal services, how much was spend on education?
A) $474,777   B) $580,283   C) $1,107,813   D) $1,424,331

275) For next year, $6,537,200 in total tax money is budgeted for all municipal services. Each category is allocated the same percentage of next year's budget as the actual percentage spent for the current year. What is the budget amount for public safety?
A) $915,208   B) $1,107,813   C) $1,372,812   D) $1,765,004

Look at the diagram below and answer questions 276 to 278.

A packaging company secures their packages with plastic strapping prior to shipment. The box is 20 inches in height, 22 inches in depth, and twenty 42 inches in length. For certain packages, 15 extra inches of strapping is used to make a handle on the top of the package to carry it. The strapping is wrapped around the length and width of the entire package, as shown in the following diagram:

276) How many inches of strapping is needed for one package, including making the handle?
   A) 124   B) 128   C) 252   D) 267

277) How many inches of strapping is needed to wrap 25 packages if no handles are used?
   A) 3,100   B) 3,200   C) 6,300   D) 6,675

278) The volume of the box must be declared prior to shipment. What is the volume in cubic inches of the box shown above?
   A) 8,800   B) 16,800   C) 18,480   D) 20,328

Look at the information below and answer questions 279 to 281.

Sam is driving a truck at 70 miles per hour. He will drive through four towns on his route: Brownsville, Dunnstun, Farnam, and Georgetown. At 10:30 am, he sees this sign:

Brownsville	**35 miles**
Dunnstun	**70 miles**
Farnam	**140 miles**
Georgetown	**210 miles**

279) After Sam sees the sign, he continues to drive at the same speed. At 11:00 am, how far will he be from Farnam?
   A) He will be in Farnam.
   B) He will be 35 miles from Farnam.
   C) He will be 70 miles from Farnam.
   D) He will be 105 miles from Farnam.

280) Where will Sam be at 12:30 pm?
   A) He will be 35 miles past Brownsville.
   B) He will be 70 miles from Farnam.
   C) He will be 70 miles from Georgetown.
   D) He will be 130 miles from Georgetown.

281)   What time will Sam arrive in Georgetown if he takes a 30 minute break in Farnam?
        A) 1:00 pm   B) 1:30 pm   C) 2:00 pm   D) 2:30 pm

Look at the bar chart below and answer questions 282 to 285.

The chart below shows data on the number of vehicles involved in accidents in Cedar Valley.

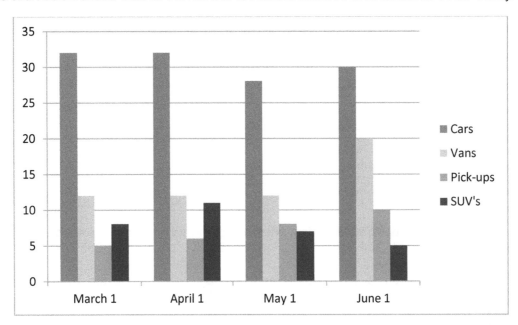

282)   Which vehicle accounted for the smallest number of accidents for May 1 and June 1 combined?
        A) Cars   B) Vans   C) Pick-ups   D) SUV's

283)   Which vehicle accounted for the largest number of accidents all four dates in total?
        A) Cars   B) Vans   C) Pick-ups   D) SUV's

284)   How many vans and SUV's were involved in accidents in Cedar Valley on March 1?
        A) 15   B) 17   C) 20   D) 37

285)   How many accidents involved pick-ups for May 1 and June 1 in total?
        A) 10   B) 11   C) 12   D) 17

Look at the information below and answer questions 286 to 288.

The journey on the Regional Railway is always exactly the same duration. The journey from Blairstown to Andersonville is the same duration as the journey from Andersonville to Blairstown.

Regional Railway Train Service from Andersonville to Blairstown	
Departure Time (Andersonville)	Arrival Time (Blairstown)
9:50 am	10:36 am
11:15 am	12:01 pm
12:30 pm	
2:15 pm	3:01 pm
	5:51 pm

286) What is the missing departure time from Andersonville in the chart above?
    A) 1:16 pm   B) 4:15 pm   C) 4:30pm   D) 5:05 pm

287) What is the missing arrival time in Blairstown in the chart above?
    A) 1:16 pm   B) 2:05 pm   C) 2:16 pm   D) 5:05 pm

288) How much travel time, excluding time spent waiting at the station, will it take to travel from
    Andersonville to Blairstown and back again to Andersonville?
    A) 46 minutes
    B) 1 hour and 22 minutes
    C) 1 hour and 32 minutes
    D) 2 hours and 32 minutes

Look at the diagram and information below and answer questions 289 to 291.

Each square in the diagram below is one yard wide and one yard long. The gray area of the diagram
represents New Town's water reservoir. The white area represents the surrounding conservation park.

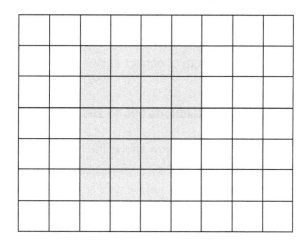

289) What is the perimeter in yards of the reservoir?
    A) 18   B) 28   C) 32   D) 63

290) What is the area in square yards of the surrounding conservation park?
    A) 18   B) 44   C) 45   D) 46

291) Which of the following ratios represents the area of the reservoir to the area of the surrounding
    conservation park?
    A) 2:5   B) 9:23   C) 17:32   D) 18:44

Look at the information below and answer questions 292 to 294.

Chantelle took a test that had four parts. The total number of questions on each part is given in the table below, as is the number of questions that Chantelle answered correctly.

Part	Total Number of Questions	Number of Questions Answered Correctly
1	15	12
2	25	20
3	35	32
4	45	32

292) How many points in total were there on parts 3 and 4 of the test?
   A) 60   B) 64   C) 70   D) 80

293) Which fraction below best represents the relationship of Chantelle's incorrect answers on Part 1 to the total points on Part 1?
   A) 1/5   B) 1/3   C) 4/5   D) 4/6

294) What was Chantelle's percentage score of correct answers for the entire test?
   A) 75%   B) 80%   C) 86%   D) 90%

Look at the bar chart below and answer questions 295 to 296.

An athlete ran 10 miles in 1.5 hours. The graph below shows the miles the athlete ran every 10 minutes.

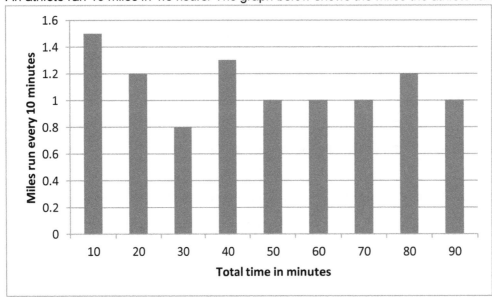

295) What was the median of the miles the athlete ran every 10 minutes for the entire race?
   A) 0.8 mile   B) 1 mile   C) 1.2 miles   D) 1.3 miles

296) What was the range of the miles the athlete ran every 10 minutes for the entire race?
   A) 0.7 mile   B) 0.8 mile   C) 1 mile   D) 1.2 miles

Look at the information below and answer questions 297 to 300.

A recipe of the ingredients needed to make 4 brownies is provided below.

Brownie recipe

¼ cup of flour
½ cup of sugar
¼ cup of butter
3 tablespoons of cocoa powder
¼ teaspoon of baking powder
½ teaspoon of vanilla extract

---

297) How much flour and sugar together is needed to double the above recipe?
A) ¾ cup
B) 1¼ cups
C) 1½ cups
D) 2 cups

298) How much sugar is needed to make 2 brownies?
A) ¼ cup
B) ¾ cup
C) 1 cup
D) 2 cups

299) How much vanilla extract is needed to make 6 brownies?
A) ¼ teaspoon
B) ¾ teaspoon
C) 1¼ teaspoons
D) 1½ teaspoons

300) How much cocoa powder and baking powder together is needed to make 12 brownies?
(1 tablespoon = 3 teaspoons)
A) 9¼ teaspoons
B) 27¼ teaspoons
C) 27½ teaspoons
D) 27¾ teaspoons

Answers to the Extra Practice Problems:

251) The correct answer is B. Bookcase A is 8 feet long and 2 feet deep, so multiply to solve: 8 × 2 = 16 square feet

252) The correct answer B. is Bookcase B is 5 feet long and two feet deep: 5 × 2 = 10 square feet

253) The correct answer is B. 70 square feet × $5.50 per piece = $385 total cost

254) The correct answer is C. Subtract the percentage of the discount from 100% to get the percentage of the price to be paid: 100% – 27.5% = 72.5%. Multiply to solve: $385 × 72.5% = $279.13

255) The correct answer is D. The total number of patients is 793,000 and 89% of them have survived, so multiply to solve: 793,000 × 0.89 = 705,770

256) The correct answer is. C. This is a more complicated question. You need to determine the death rate, so subtract the survival rate from 100% to get the death rate for each category. Then multiply for each category and compare:
Cardiopulmonary and vascular deaths: 602,000 × 0.18 = 108,360
HIV/AIDS deaths: 215,000 × 0.27 = 58,050
Diabetes deaths: 793,000 × 0.11 = 87,230
Cancer and leukemia deaths: 231,000 × 0.52 =120,120
Deaths from premature birth complications: 68,000 × 0.36 = 24,480
So cancer and leukemia caused the greatest number of deaths.

257) The correct answer is A. Refer to your calculations for question 7 and add the two smallest amounts together: 24,480 + 58,050 = 82,530

258) The correct answer is B. The line with the squares is the highest line for July. From the legend, we can see that this represents Company B.

259) The correct answer is C. The line with the diamonds represents Company A. The diamond symbol for April is nearly at the line for 8. The sales are represented in hundreds of thousands, so $790,000 is the best answer.

260) The correct answer is A. The line with the square for company B is at $1,400,000 for May. The line with the triangle for Company C is at $600,000 for May. So, Company B's sales were $800,000 more than Company C's for May.

261) The correct answer is A. We can see that December has the highest figure for all three of the lines. Accordingly, December will also have the greatest combined sales for all three companies.

262) The correct answer is C. Cobb County is the darkest bar, so it is the first bar for each month. For July, Cobb County had 1.2 inches of rain, and in August it had 0.8 inches, so it had 2 inches in total for the two months.

263) The correct answer is B. In June, Dawson County had 1.1 inches of rain and Emery County had 1.7 inches. Therefore, Emery County had 0.6 more inches of rainfall than Dawson County.

264) The correct answer is A. Emery County had the following amounts of rainfall: May = 2.5 inches; June = 1.8 inches; July = 1 inch; August = 0.9 inch. Then add these amounts together to solve: 2.5 + 1.8 + 1 + 0.9 = 6.2 inches in total

265) The correct answer is D. Reptiles account for 42% of the zoo creatures, and there are 1,500 creatures in total, so multiply to solve: 1,500 × 0.42 = 630 reptiles

266) The correct answer is B. At the start of the year, 26% of the zoo creatures were quadrupeds and 15% of the creatures were fish. So, solve by multiplying and subtracting as follows: (1500 × 0.26) − (1500 × 0.15) = 390 − 225 = 165 more quadrupeds than fish

267) The correct answer is C. We have to calculate the percentage of birds at the start of the year by subtracting the percentages for the other categories: 100% − 40% − 21% − 16% = 23%. The percentage of birds was 17% at the start of the year and 23% at the end of the year, so there was a 6% increase in the bird population. We can then multiply to solve: 1,500 × 0.06 = 90 more birds at the end of the year

268) The correct answer is A. The temperature on Sunday was −10 and on Saturday is was 12, so we calculate the difference by subtracting Sunday from Saturday: 12 − (−10) = 12 + 10 = 22 degrees

269) The correct answer is C. Place the values for the temperatures in ascending order: −10, −9, 1, 6, 8, 12, 13. The median is the one in the middle: −10, −9, 1 , **6** , 8, 12, 13

270) The correct answer is B. Add up all of the values: −10 + −9 + 1 + 6 + 8 + 12 + 13 = 21. Then divide by 7 for the seven days represented: 21 ÷ 7 = 3

271) The correct answer is D. None of the values occurs more than once, so there is no mode.

272) The correct answer is D. The range is the high minus the low: 13 − (−10) = 23

273) The correct answer is B. The health and other categories were the lowest, so add them together to solve: 11% + 9% = 20%

274) The correct answer is D. Take the total dollar amount and multiply by the 27% for education: $5,275,300 × 0.27 = $1,424,331

275) The correct answer is C. Take the total dollar amount of the budget and multiply by the 21% for public safety: $6,537,200 × 0.21 = $1,372,812

276) The correct answer is D. Calculate the length of strapping for the piece that goes over the front of the package: 22 + 42 + 22 + 42 = 128. Then calculate the length of strapping for the piece that goes over the top of the package: 20 + 42 + 20 + 42 = 124. Then add the 15 inches for the handle: 128 + 124 + 15 = 267 total inches

277) The correct answer is C. Without the handle, we need 128 + 124 = 252 inches per package. 252 inches per package × 25 packages = 6,300 total inches

278) The correct answer is C. To calculate cubic inches, we take the height times the depth times the length: 20 × 22 × 42 = 18,480 cubic inches

279) The correct answer is D. At 11:00, thirty minutes (or half an hour) will have passed. If he is traveling 70 miles per hour, he will have traveled 35 miles in this half hour (70 × ½ = 35). If he was 140 miles from Farnam when he saw the sign, we need to subtract 35 miles from this to get the answer: 140 − 35 = 105 miles from Farnam

280) The correct answer is C. At 12:30, two hours will have passed and he will have traveled 140 miles (70 miles per hour × 2 hours = 140 total miles). Georgetown was 210 miles away when he saw the sign, so subtract to find out how far he is from Georgetown: 210 − 140 = 70 miles from Georgetown

281) The correct answer is C. From the previous question, we know that at 12:30 he is 70 miles from Georgetown without having taken a break. If he is traveling 70 miles per hour, he would need only 1 more hour to get to Georgetown at 1:30 if he had not taken a break. But we need to add in a 30 minute break, so he would arrive in Georgetown at 2:00 pm.

282) The correct answer is D. We can see that SUV's account for the lowest number of accidents on each of the two dates. So, SUV's will also account for the lowest combined total for the two dates.

283) The correct answer is A. The chart shows that cars account for the largest number of accidents on each of the four dates represented. So, cars will also account for the largest combined total for all four dates.

284) The correct answer is C. Vans were involved in 12 accidents on March 1, and SUV's were involved in 8 accidents on the same date. So, vans and SUV's had 20 accidents in total on this date.

285) The correct answer is D. On May 1, pick-ups were involved in 7 accidents, and on June 1, they were involved in 10 accidents. So, for the two dates combined, pick-ups had 17 accidents.

286) The correct answer is D. Each journey lasts 46 minutes, so if the train arrives at 5:51 pm, it departs at 5:05 pm. (5:51 − 46 minutes = 5:05)

287) The correct answer is A. Each journey lasts 46 minutes, so if the train departs at 12:30 pm, it will arrive at 1:16 pm. (12:30 + 46 minutes = 1:16)

288) The correct answer is C. It is 46 minutes there and 46 minutes back, so the travel time for a round trip is 46 + 46 = 92 minutes, which is 1 hour and 32 minutes.

289) The correct answer is A. Count the sides of the squares on the gray part of the diagram: Left = 5; Bottom = 3 + 1 = 4, Right = 2 + 3 = 5; Top = 4. Then add up: 5 + 4 + 5 + 4 = 18. Alternatively, visually go around the gray figure and count up the outside edges of the gray squares.

290) The correct answer is C. First, calculate the total area represented on the diagram: 9 × 7 = 63 square yards in total. Then count the gray squares for the reservoir. We can see that there are 18 gray squares. Then subtract to solve: 63 – 18 = 45 square yards

291) The correct answer is A. We know from the calculations in the previous question that the gray area is 18 square yards and the white area is 45 square yards. So, the ratio is 18:45. Both of these numbers are divisible by 9, so we can simplify the ratio to 2:5 (18 ÷ 9 = 2 and 45 ÷ 9 = 5)

292) The correct answer is D. Part 3 had 35 total questions and part 4 had 45 total questions, so add to solve: 35 + 45 = 80

293) The correct answer is A. Chantelle correctly answered 12 out of 15 questions, so she incorrectly answered 3 questions (15 – 12 = 3). This can be expressed as the fraction 3/15, which can be simplified to 1/5.

294) The correct answer is B. First calculate how many correct answers there were: 12 + 20 + 32 + 32 = 96. Then calculate how many questions were on the test in total: 15 + 25 + 35 + 45 = 120. Finally, divide to solve 96 ÷ 120 = 0.80 = 80%

295) The correct answer is B. The median is the middle value when the values in the data set are in ascending order. So, put the values in ascending order first of all: 0.8, 1, 1, 1, 1, 1.2, 1.2, 1.3, 1.5. The median is the one in the middle: 0.8, 1, 1, 1, **1**, 1.2, 1.2, 1.3, 1.5

296) The correct answer is A. The range is the highest value minus the lowest value: 1.5 – 0.8 = 0.7

297) The correct answer is C. For one recipe, we need ¼ cup of flour and ½ cup of sugar, which is equal to ¾ when combined. We are doubling the recipe, so we need ¾ × 2 = 1½ cups.

298) The correct answer is A. The recipe is for 4 brownies, but we only want to make 2 brownies, so we have to use half of the ingredients. ½ cup of sugar is needed for the original recipe, but we only want half of this: ½ × ½ = ¼

299) The correct answer is B. The original recipe was for 4 brownies but we are making 6 brownies, so we can set up the following fraction to get our proportion: 6/4 = 4/4 + 2/4 = 1 + ½ = 1½. So for 6 brownies, we need to use 1½ of all of the ingredients listed on the original recipe: ½ teaspoon × 1½ = [(½ × 1) + (½ × ½)] = ½ + ¼ = ¾

300) The correct answer is D. 3 tablespoons of cocoa powder and ¼ teaspoon of baking powder are needed for the original recipe to make 4 brownies. There are 3 teaspoons in a tablespoon, so calculate the total teaspoons needed for the original recipe first: 3 tablespoons × 3 = 9 teaspoons cocoa powder + ¼ teaspoon baking powder = 9¼ teaspoons in total. We are now making 12 brownies, so we need to multiply all of the ingredients by 3: 9¼ × 3 = 27¾ teaspoons

ANSWER KEY

1)	D	27)	C
2)	D	28)	B
3)	A	29)	D
4)	B	30)	A
5)	A	31)	D
6)	B	32)	C
7)	B	33)	D
8)	D	34)	C
9)	B	35)	C
10)	C	36)	C
11)	C	37)	B
12)	D	38)	D
13)	A	39)	A
14)	B	40)	A
15)	D	41)	A
16)	C	42)	D
17)	C	43)	A
18)	D	44)	B
19)	A	45)	C
20)	D	46)	B
21)	B	47)	C
22)	D	48)	A
23)	C	49)	C
24)	D	50)	B
25)	A	51)	B
26)	B	52)	B

53) A		80) D	
54) A		81) C	
55) C		82) C	
56) A		83) B	
57) B		84) C	
58) C		85) A	
59) B		86) A	
60) D		87) D	
61) D		88) C	
62) D		89) D	
63) C		90) C	
64) B		91) A	
65) C		92) A	
66) D		93) D	
67) D		94) B	
68) C		95) D	
69) A		96) B	
70) C		97) C	
71) D		98) A	
72) C		99) B	
73) D		100) D	
74) D		101) A	
75) D		102) C	
76) C		103) D	
77) B		104) D	
78) A		105) A	
79) A		106) D	

107) A	134) D
108) B	135) C
109) B	136) C
110) B	137) B
111) A	138) B
112) D	139) A
113) A	140) D
114) A	141) B
115) C	142) C
116) D	143) B
117) A	144) A
118) C	145) A
119) B	146) D
120) B	147) C
121) D	148) D
122) D	149) B
123) D	150) D
124) A	151) A
125) B	152) C
126) B	153) B
127) C	154) A
128) A	155) A
129) D	156) C
130) C	157) B
131) D	158) D
132) A	159) C
133) A	160) A

161) D	188) A
162) B	189) B
163) D	190) C
164) D	191) A
165) B	192) C
166) C	193) B
167) A	194) A
168) A	195) D
169) D	196) C
170) B	197) C
171) B	198) D
172) A	199) D
173) C	200) D
174) C	201) C
175) A	202) A
176) D	203) C
177) C	204) B
178) B	205) C
179) A	206) B
180) A	207) B
181) B	208) D
182) D	209) D
183) D	210) D
184) D	211) D
185) C	212) C
186) D	213) D
187) C	214) C

215) C

216) D

217) C

218) B

219) B

220) A

221) B

222) A

223) D

224) C

225) C

226) B

227) B

228) A

229) C

230) C

231) B

232) B

233) C

234) A

235) D

236) C

237) D

238) C

239) C

240) D

241) C

242) A

243) C

244) B

245) A

246) A

247) C

248) D

249) D

250) B

251) B

252) B

253) B

254) C

255) D

256) C

257) A

258) B

259) C

260) A

261) A

262) C

263) B

264) A

265) D

266) B

267) C

268) A

269)	C		285)	D
270)	B		286)	D
271)	D		287)	A
272)	D		288)	C
273)	B		289)	A
274)	D		290)	C
275)	C		291)	A
276)	D		292)	D
277)	C		293)	A
278)	C		294)	B
279)	D		295)	B
280)	C		296)	A
281)	C		297)	C
282)	D		298)	A
283)	A		299)	B
284)	C		300)	D

CPSIA information can be obtained
at www.ICGtesting.com
Printed in the USA
LVHW060207140422
716188LV00018B/199